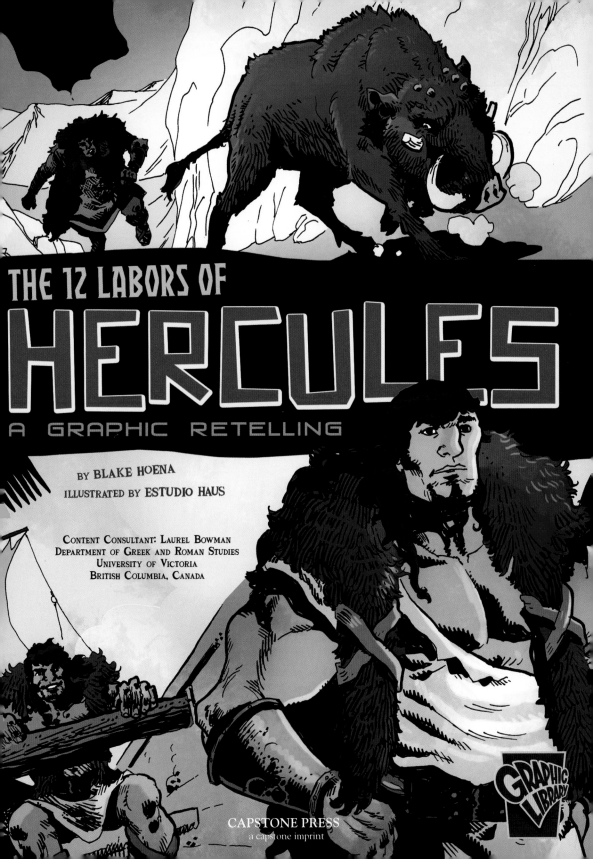

THE 12 LABORS OF
HERCULES
A GRAPHIC RETELLING

BY BLAKE HOENA

ILLUSTRATED BY ESTUDIO HAUS

CONTENT CONSULTANT: LAUREL BOWMAN
DEPARTMENT OF GREEK AND ROMAN STUDIES
UNIVERSITY OF VICTORIA
BRITISH COLUMBIA, CANADA

CAPSTONE PRESS
a capstone imprint

Graphic Library is published by Capstone Press,
1710 Roe Crest Drive, North Mankato, Minnesota 56003
www.capstonepub.com

Library of Congress Cataloging-in-Publication Data
Hoena, B. A., author.
   The 12 labors of Hercules : a graphic retelling / by Blake Hoena ; illustrated by Estudio Haus.
       pages cm.—(Graphic library. Ancient myths)
   Summary: "The story of Hercules and his 12 labors told in graphic novel format"—Provided by
publisher.
   Audience: Ages 8-14.
   Audience: Grades 4 to 6.
   Includes bibliographical references and index.
   ISBN 978-1-4914-2071-3 (library binding)
   ISBN 978-1-4914-2275-5 (paperback)
   ISBN 978-1-4914-2289-2 (ebook pdf)
1. Heracles (Greek mythology)—Comic books, strips, etc. 2. Heracles (Greek mythology)—Juvenile
literature. 3. Hercules (Roman mythology)—Comic books, strips, etc. 4. Hercules (Roman mythology)—
Juvenile literature. 5. Mythology, Classical—Comic books, strips, etc. 6. Mythology, Classical—Juvenile
literature. I. Estudio Haus (Firm), illustrator. II. Title. III. Title: Twelve labors of Hercules.
   BL820.H5H64 2015
   398.2'0938—dc23   2014019186

Editor
Anthony Wacholtz

Art Director
Nathan Gassman

Designer
Ashlee Suker

Production Specialist
Tori Abraham

Printed in the United States of America in Stevens Point, Wisconsin
092014   008479WZS15

TABLE OF CONTENTS

ORIGINS OF THE MYTH

Heracles was a mighty hero in Greek myths. But in modern stories, his Roman name—Hercules—is used more often. This adaptation of Hercules' story is based on the book *The Library*, written by Greek historian Apollodorus.

CHAPTER ONE

THE ORACLE OF DELPHI

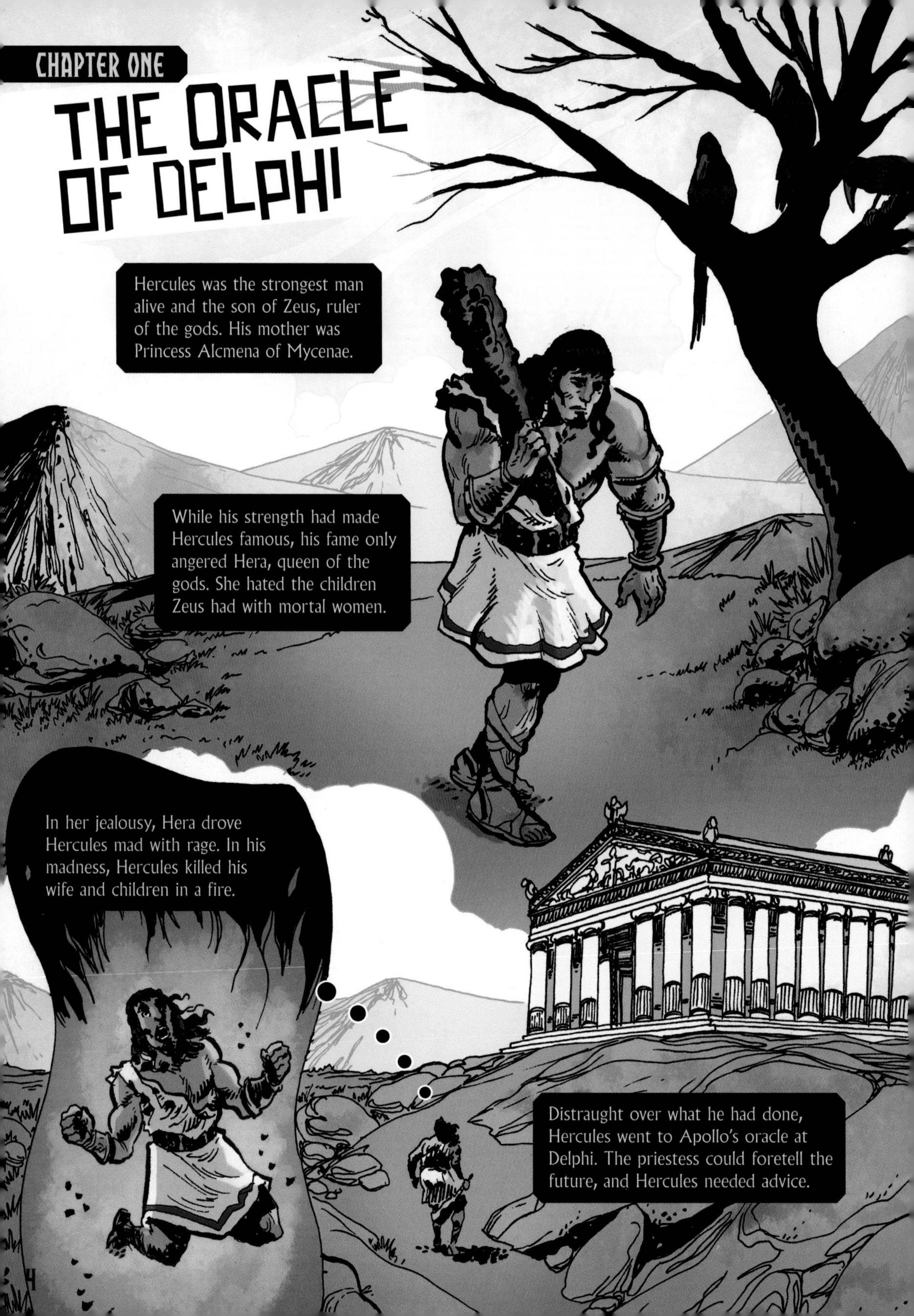
Hercules was the strongest man alive and the son of Zeus, ruler of the gods. His mother was Princess Alcmena of Mycenae.
While his strength had made Hercules famous, his fame only angered Hera, queen of the gods. She hated the children Zeus had with mortal women.
In her jealousy, Hera drove Hercules mad with rage. In his madness, Hercules killed his wife and children in a fire.
Distraught over what he had done, Hercules went to Apollo's oracle at Delphi. The priestess could foretell the future, and Hercules needed advice.

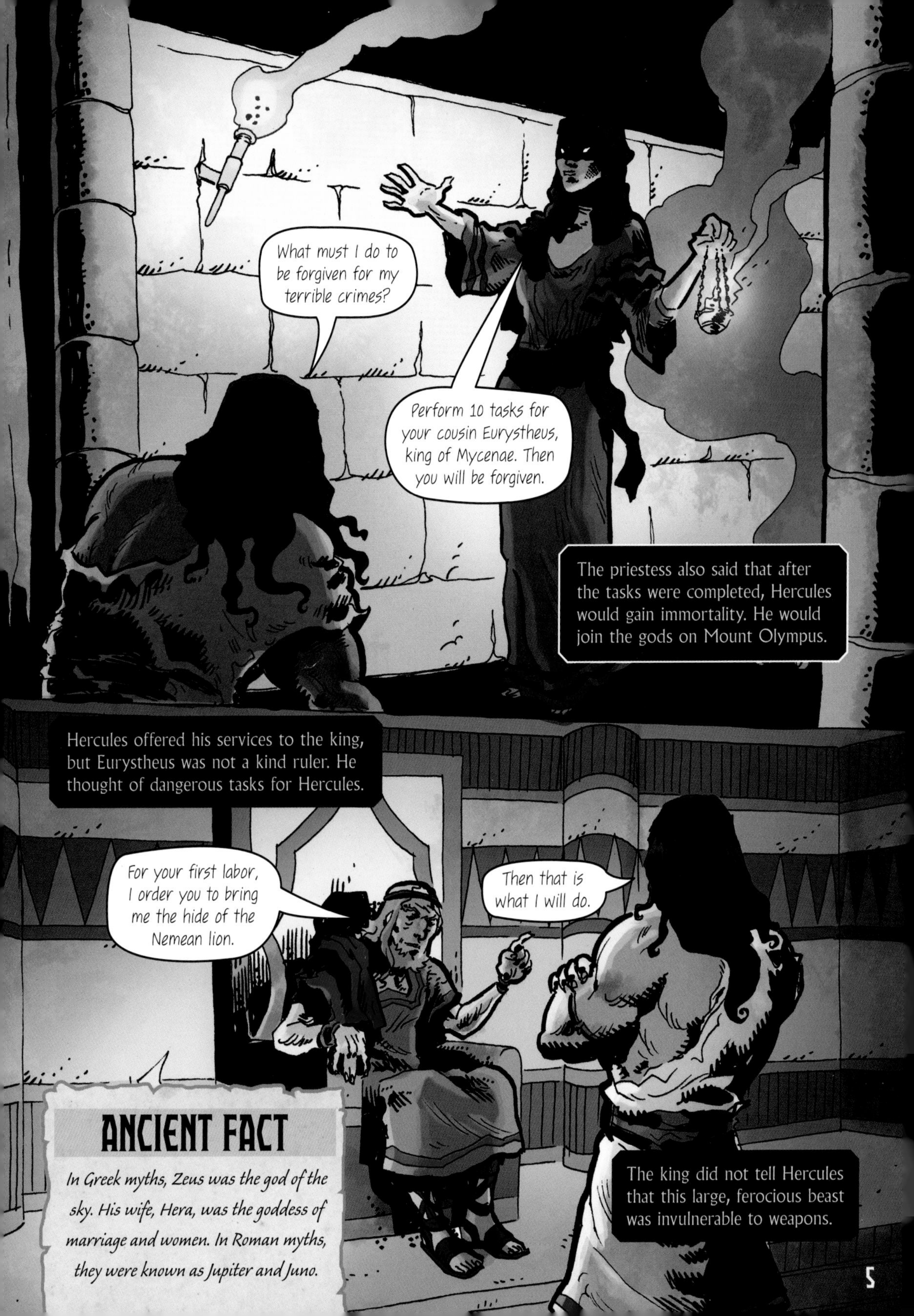
What must I do to be forgiven for my terrible crimes?
Perform 10 tasks for your cousin Eurystheus, king of Mycenae. Then you will be forgiven.
The priestess also said that after the tasks were completed, Hercules would gain immortality. He would join the gods on Mount Olympus.
Hercules offered his services to the king, but Eurystheus was not a kind ruler. He thought of dangerous tasks for Hercules.
For your first labor, I order you to bring me the hide of the Nemean lion.
Then that is what I will do.
The king did not tell Hercules that this large, ferocious beast was invulnerable to weapons.

ANCIENT FACT

In Greek myths, Zeus was the god of the sky. His wife, Hera, was the goddess of marriage and women. In Roman myths, they were known as Jupiter and Juno.

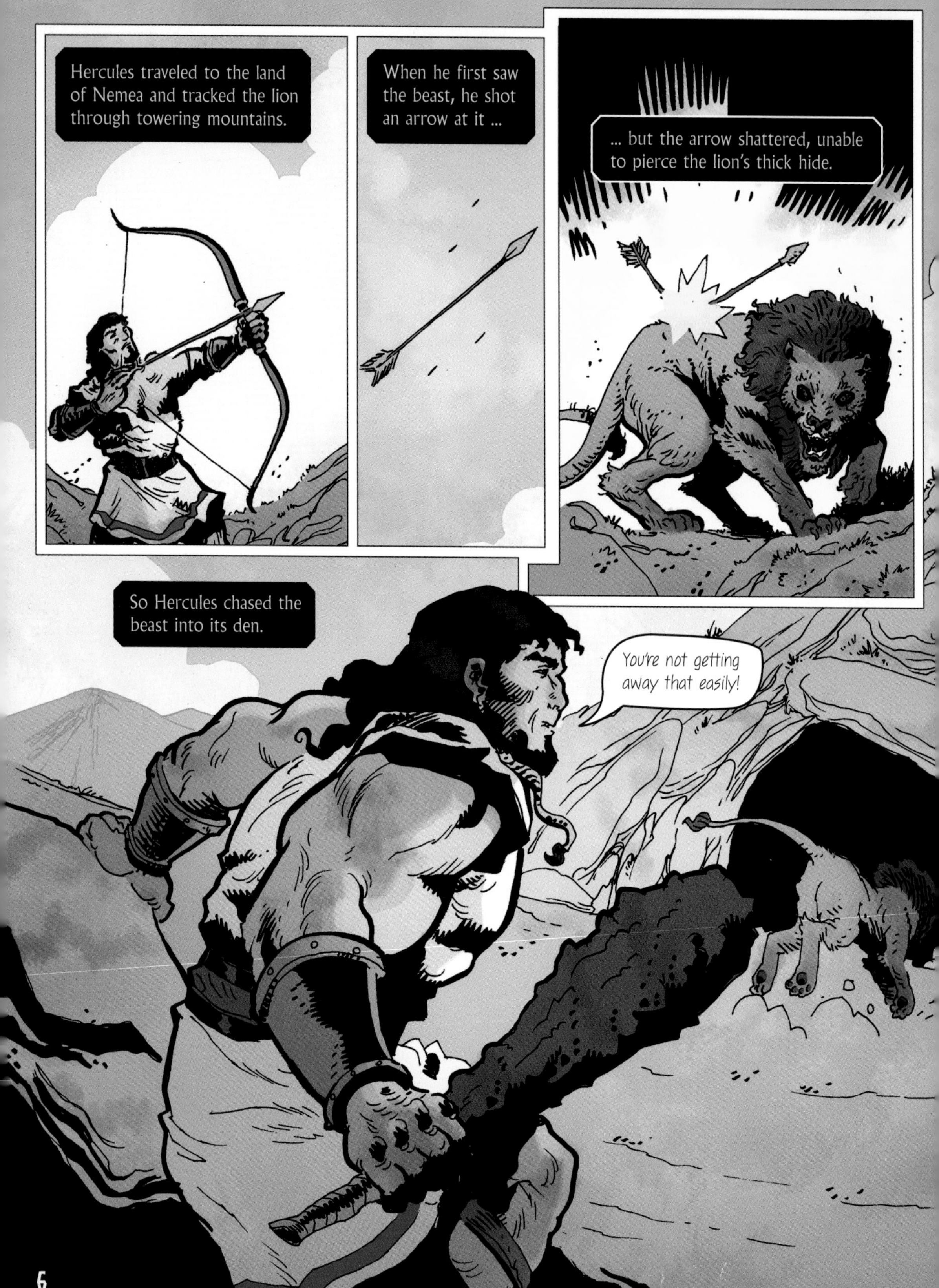
Hercules traveled to the land of Nemea and tracked the lion through towering mountains.
When he first saw the beast, he shot an arrow at it ...
... but the arrow shattered, unable to pierce the lion's thick hide.
So Hercules chased the beast into its den.
You're not getting away that easily!

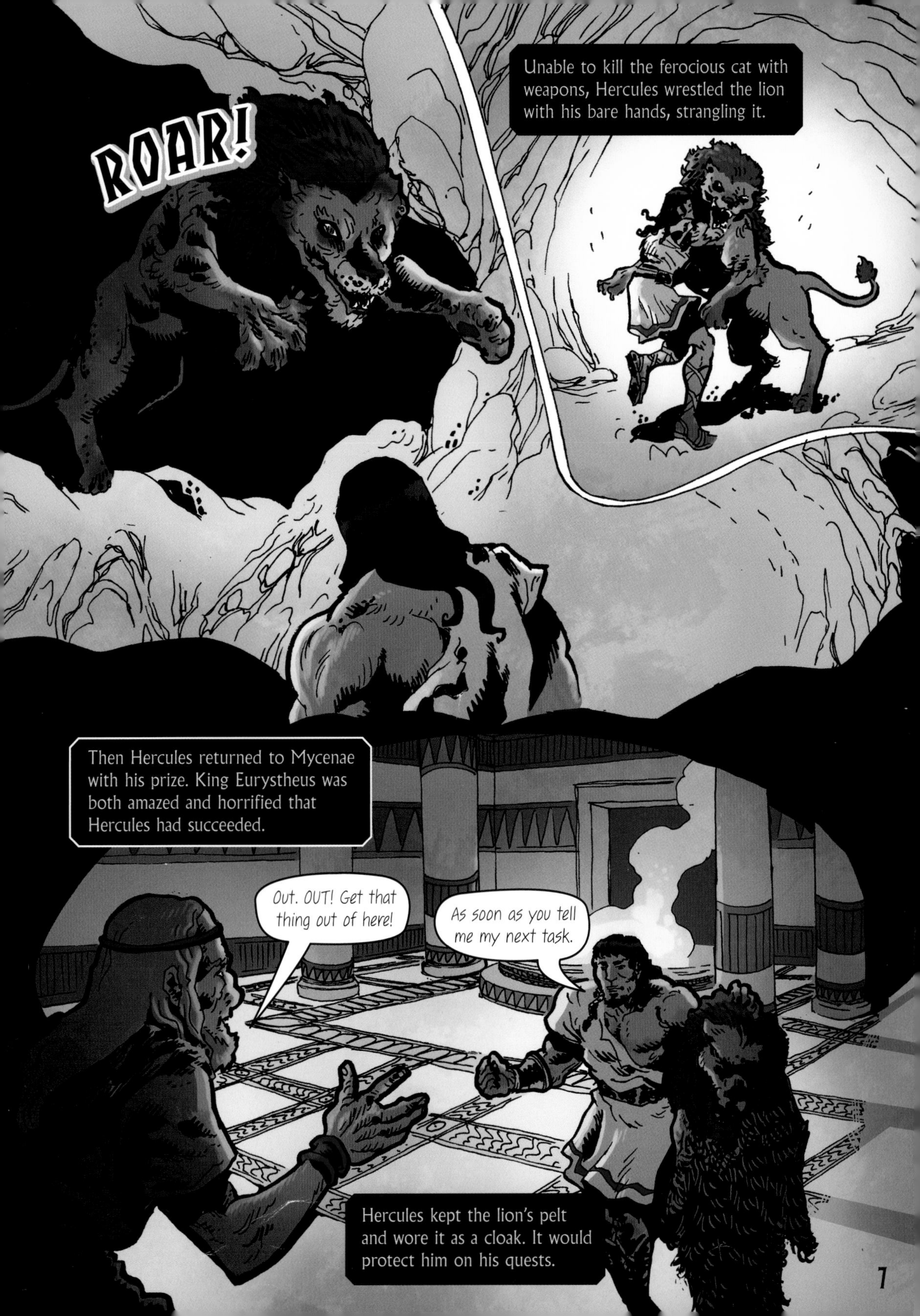
ROAR!
Unable to kill the ferocious cat with weapons, Hercules wrestled the lion with his bare hands, strangling it.
Then Hercules returned to Mycenae with his prize. King Eurystheus was both amazed and horrified that Hercules had succeeded.
Out. OUT! Get that thing out of here!
As soon as you tell me my next task.
Hercules kept the lion's pelt and wore it as a cloak. It would protect him on his quests.

CHAPTER TWO
THE EARLY LABORS

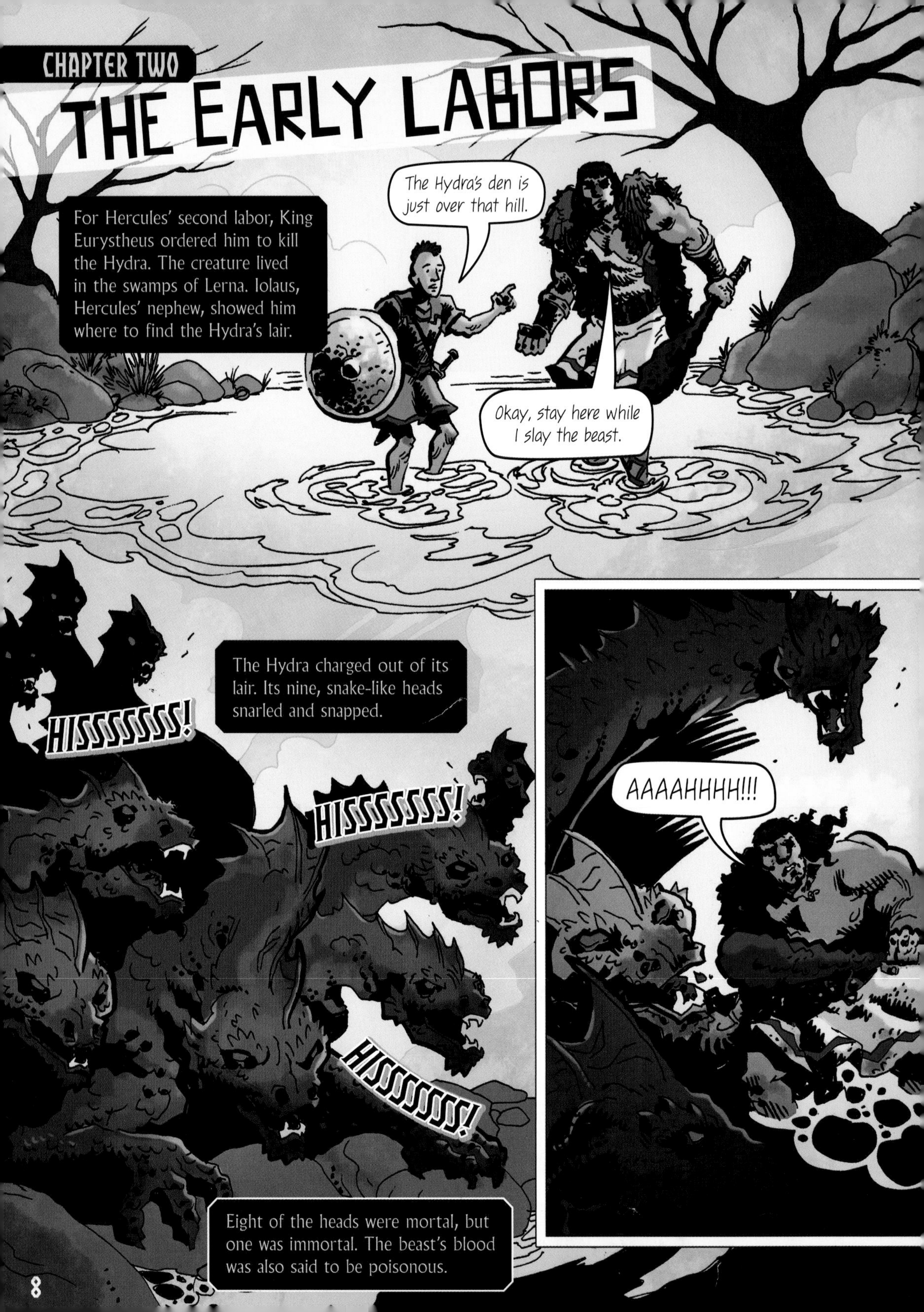

For Hercules' second labor, King Eurystheus ordered him to kill the Hydra. The creature lived in the swamps of Lerna. Iolaus, Hercules' nephew, showed him where to find the Hydra's lair.
The Hydra's den is just over that hill.
Okay, stay here while I slay the beast.
The Hydra charged out of its lair. Its nine, snake-like heads snarled and snapped.
HISSSSSSSS!
HISSSSSSSS!
HISSSSSSSS!
Eight of the heads were mortal, but one was immortal. The beast's blood was also said to be poisonous.
AAAAHHHH!!!

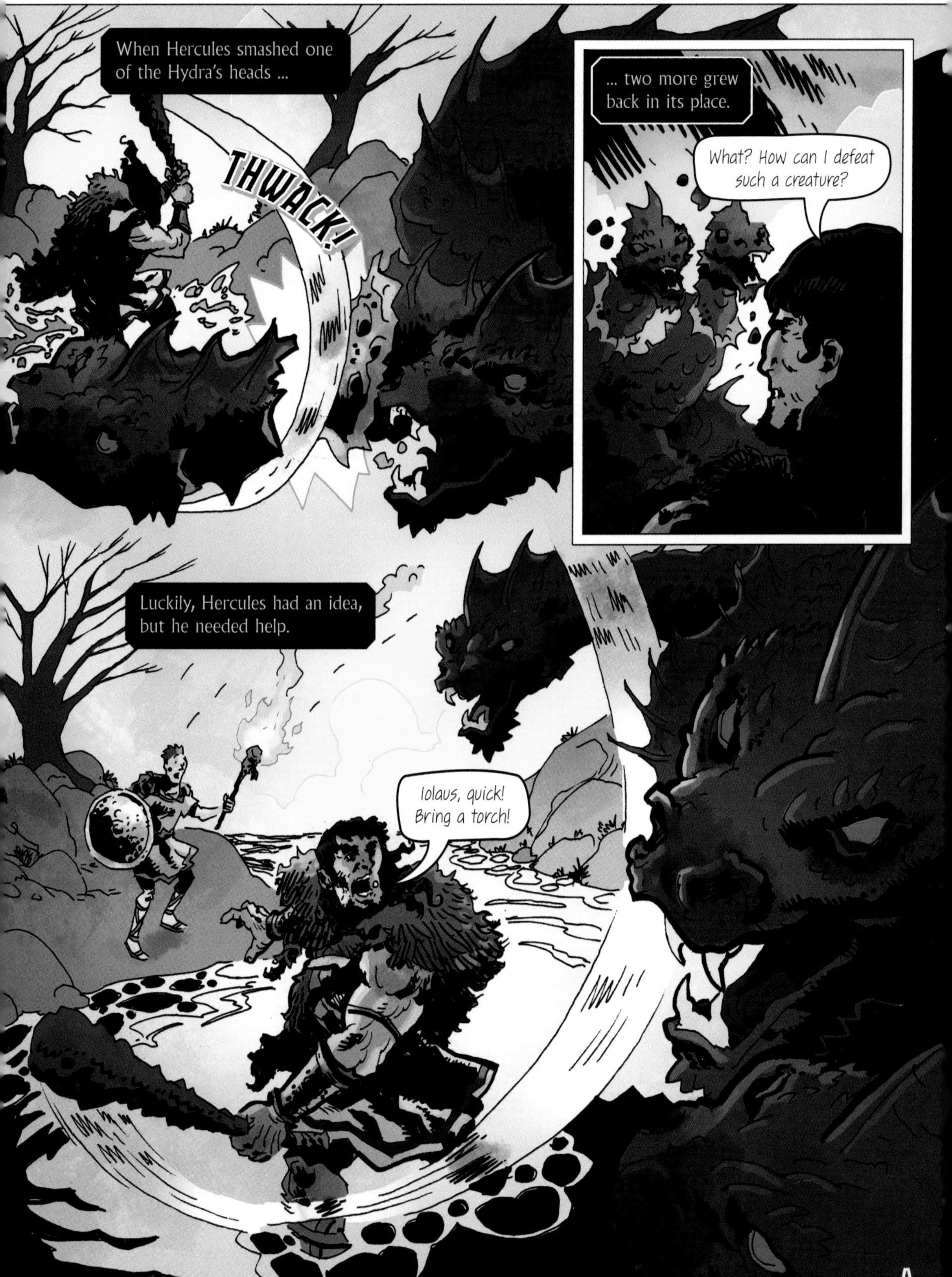

When Hercules smashed one of the Hydra's heads ...
THWACK!
... two more grew back in its place.
What? How can I defeat such a creature?
Luckily, Hercules had an idea, but he needed help.
Iolaus, quick! Bring a torch!

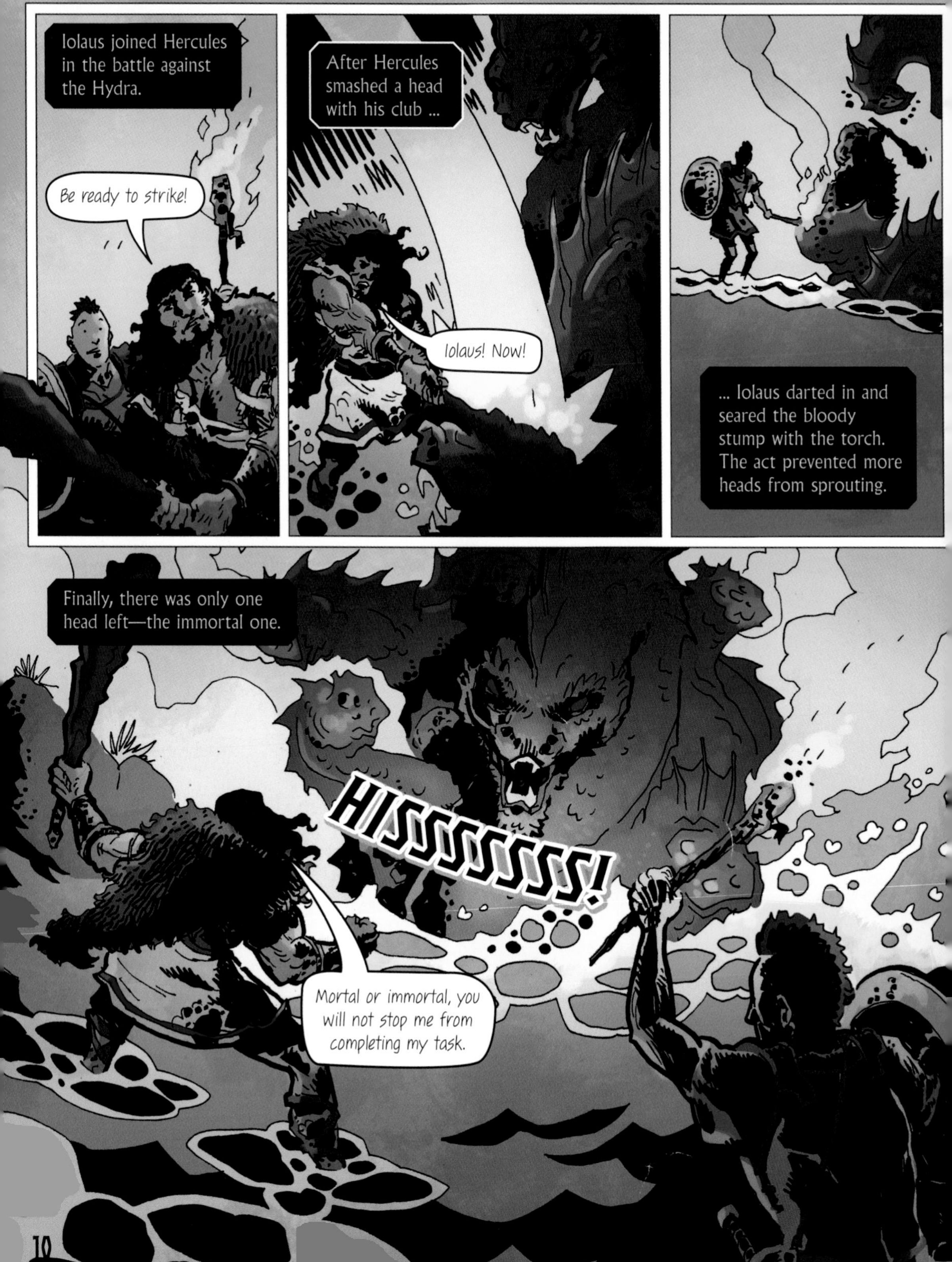
Iolaus joined Hercules in the battle against the Hydra.
Be ready to strike!
After Hercules smashed a head with his club ...
Iolaus! Now!
... Iolaus darted in and seared the bloody stump with the torch. The act prevented more heads from sprouting.
Finally, there was only one head left—the immortal one.
HISSSSSSSS!
Mortal or immortal, you will not stop me from completing my task.

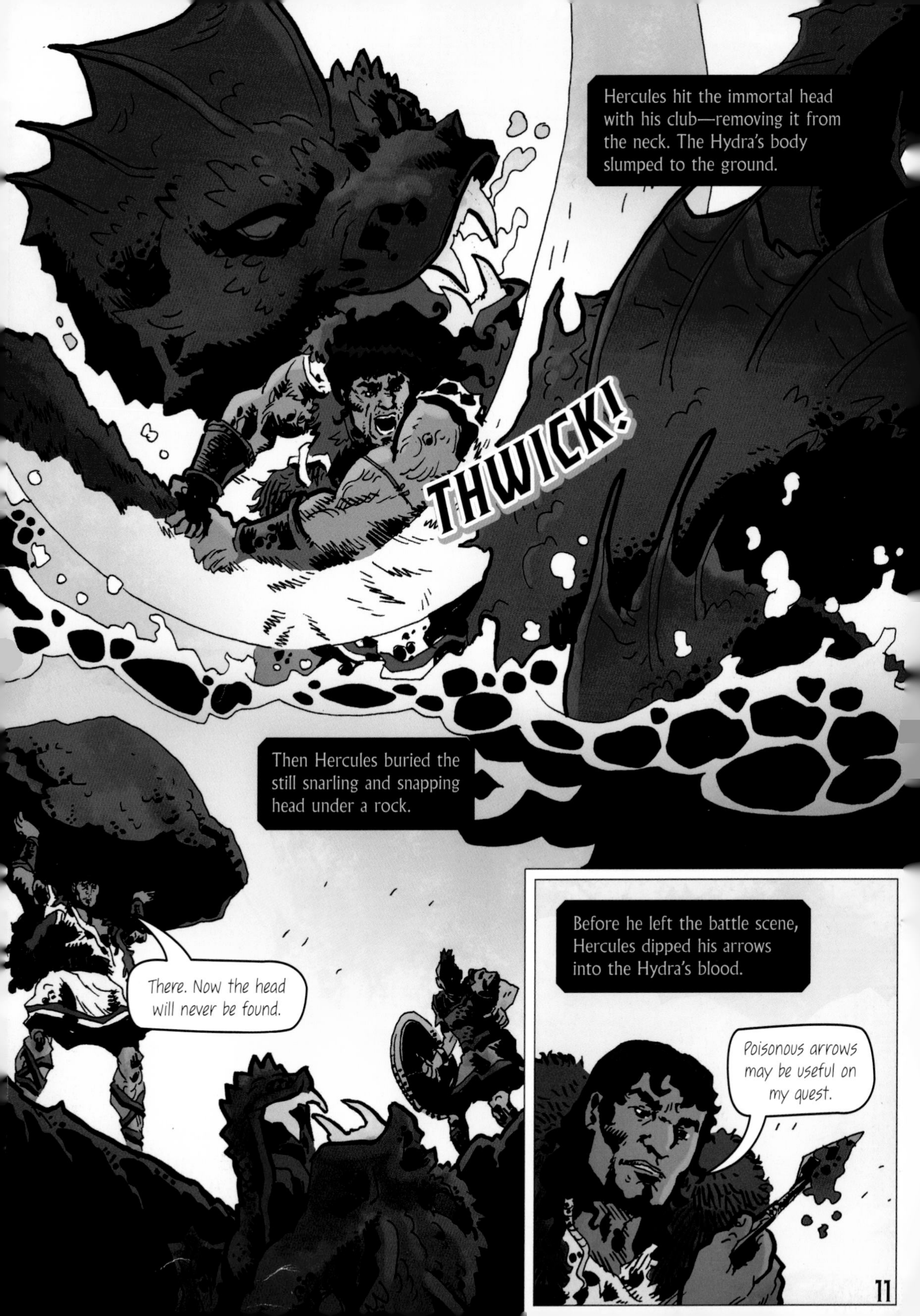

Hercules hit the immortal head with his club—removing it from the neck. The Hydra's body slumped to the ground.
THWICK!
Then Hercules buried the still snarling and snapping head under a rock.
There. Now the head will never be found.
Before he left the battle scene, Hercules dipped his arrows into the Hydra's blood.
Poisonous arrows may be useful on my quest.

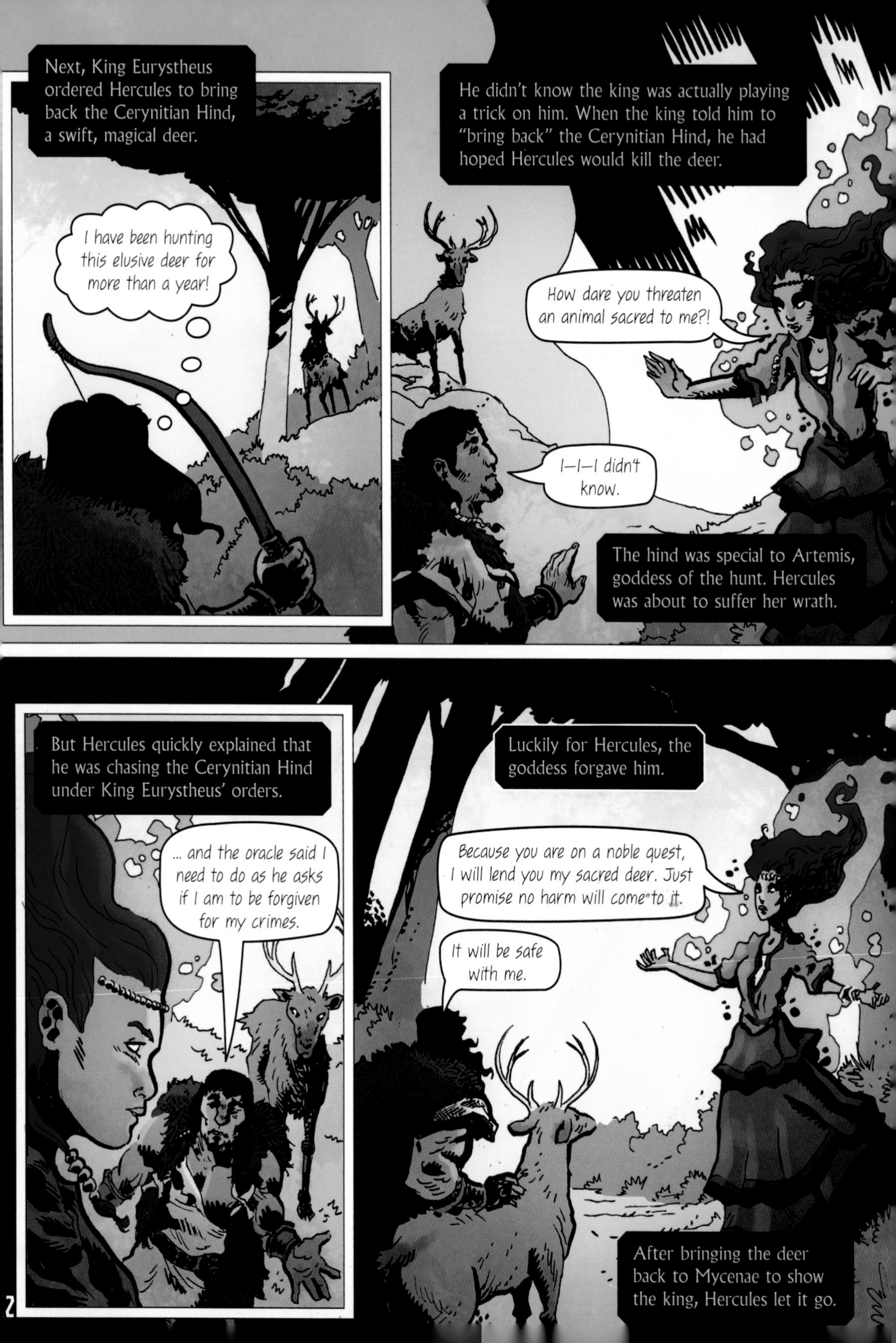
Next, King Eurystheus ordered Hercules to bring back the Cerynitian Hind, a swift, magical deer.
I have been hunting this elusive deer for more than a year!
He didn't know the king was actually playing a trick on him. When the king told him to "bring back" the Cerynitian Hind, he had hoped Hercules would kill the deer.
How dare you threaten an animal sacred to me?!
I—I—I didn't know.
The hind was special to Artemis, goddess of the hunt. Hercules was about to suffer her wrath.
But Hercules quickly explained that he was chasing the Cerynitian Hind under King Eurystheus' orders.
... and the oracle said I need to do as he asks if I am to be forgiven for my crimes.
Luckily for Hercules, the goddess forgave him.
Because you are on a noble quest, I will lend you my sacred deer. Just promise no harm will come to it.
It will be safe with me.
After bringing the deer back to Mycenae to show the king, Hercules let it go.

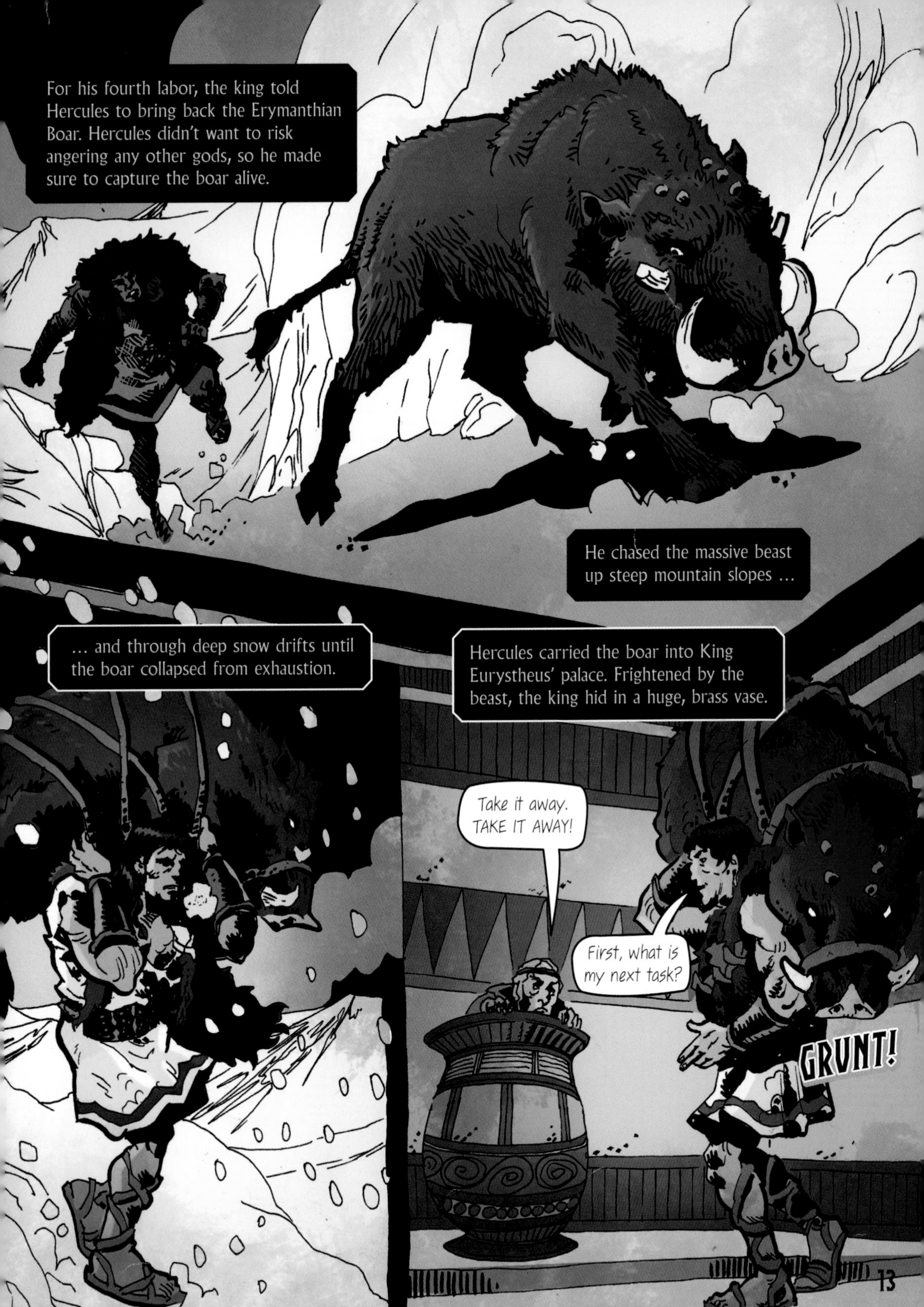
For his fourth labor, the king told Hercules to bring back the Erymanthian Boar. Hercules didn't want to risk angering any other gods, so he made sure to capture the boar alive.
He chased the massive beast up steep mountain slopes ...
... and through deep snow drifts until the boar collapsed from exhaustion.
Hercules carried the boar into King Eurystheus' palace. Frightened by the beast, the king hid in a huge, brass vase.
Take it away. TAKE IT AWAY!
First, what is my next task?
GRUNT!

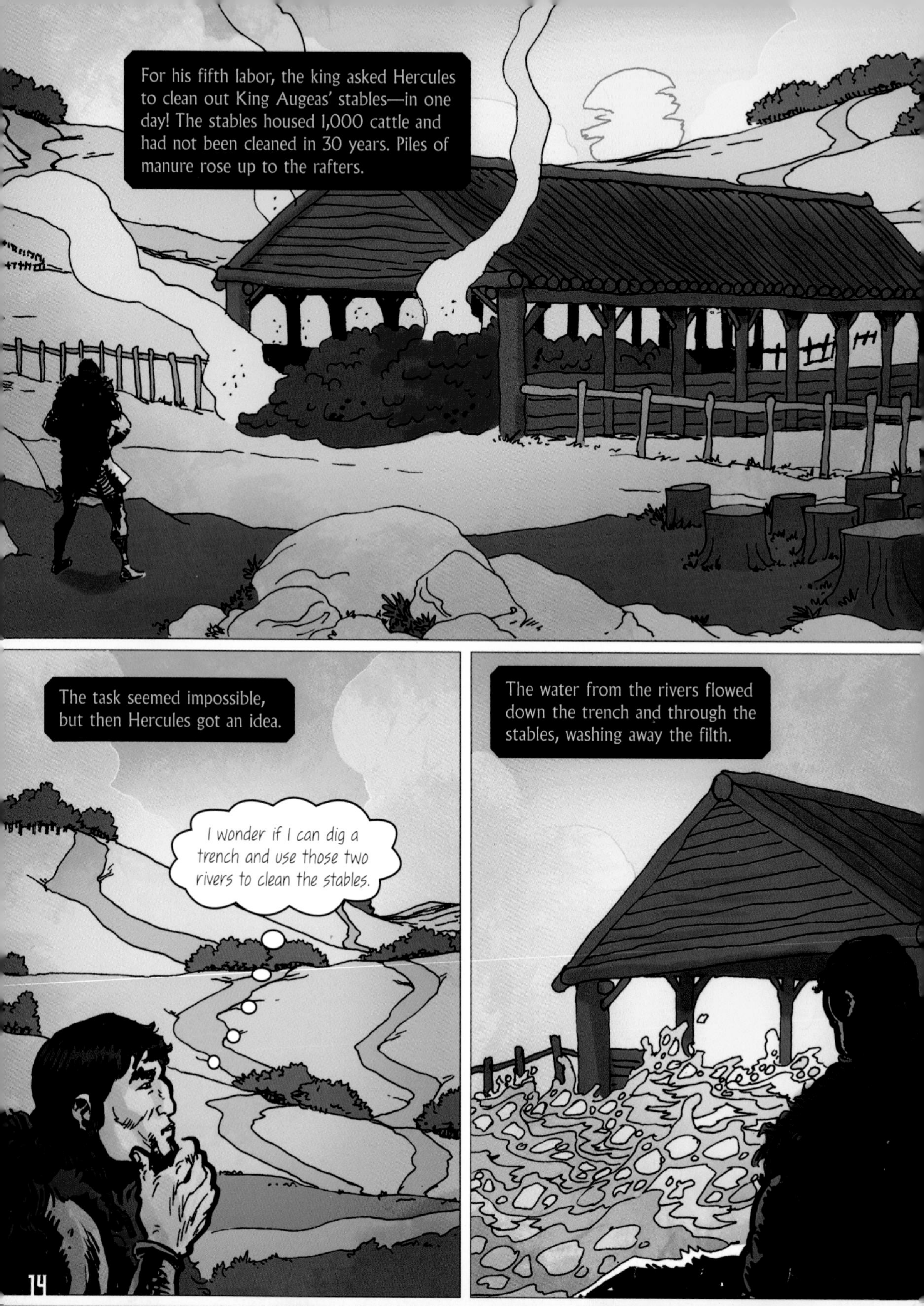
For his fifth labor, the king asked Hercules to clean out King Augeas' stables—in one day! The stables housed 1,000 cattle and had not been cleaned in 30 years. Piles of manure rose up to the rafters.
The task seemed impossible, but then Hercules got an idea.
I wonder if I can dig a trench and use those two rivers to clean the stables.
The water from the rivers flowed down the trench and through the stables, washing away the filth.

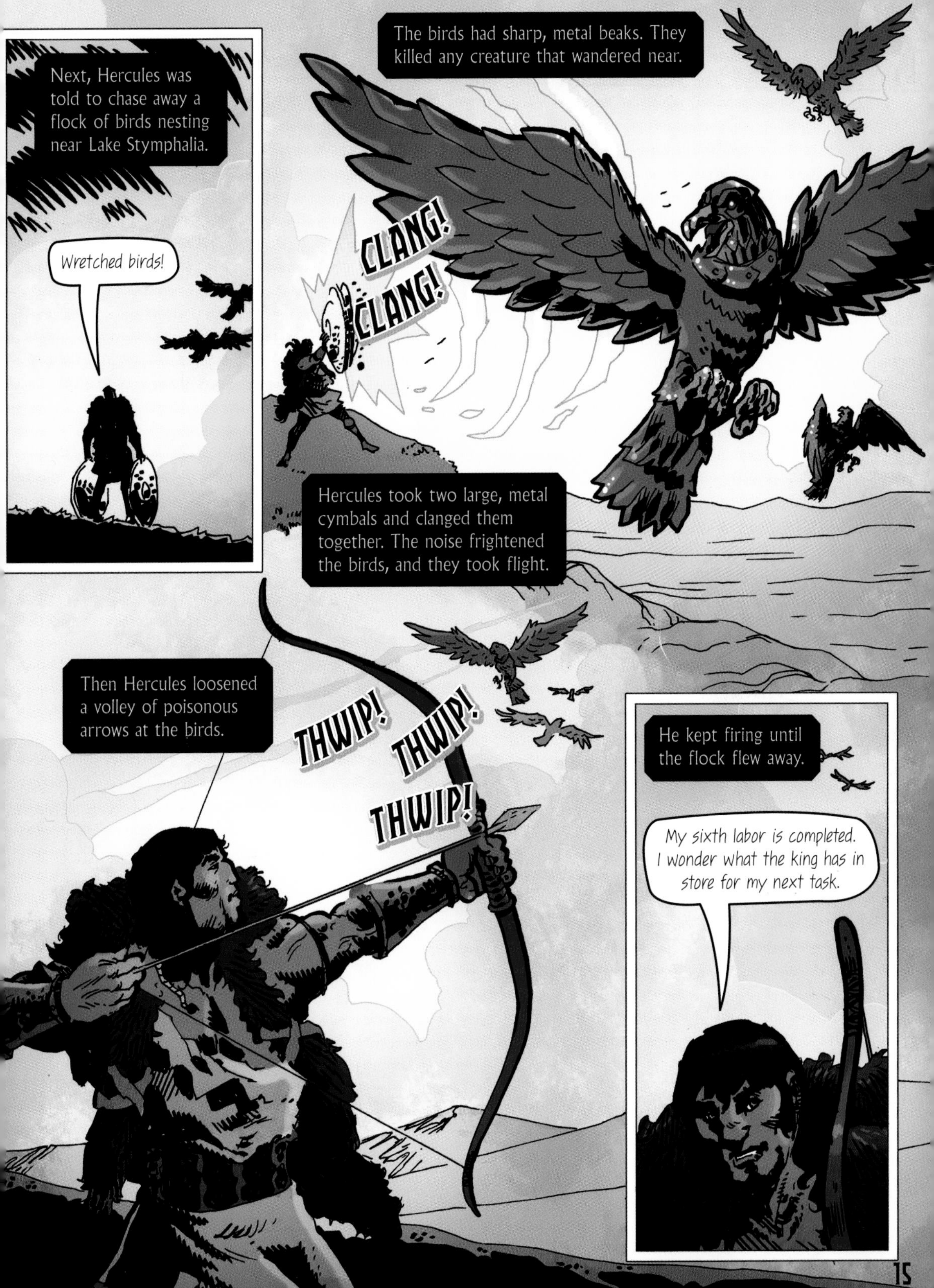
Next, Hercules was told to chase away a flock of birds nesting near Lake Stymphalia.
Wretched birds!
The birds had sharp, metal beaks. They killed any creature that wandered near.
CLANG!
CLANG!
Hercules took two large, metal cymbals and clanged them together. The noise frightened the birds, and they took flight.
Then Hercules loosened a volley of poisonous arrows at the birds.
THWIP!
THWIP!
THWIP!
He kept firing until the flock flew away.
My sixth labor is completed. I wonder what the king has in store for my next task.

CHAPTER THREE

THE MIDDLE LABORS

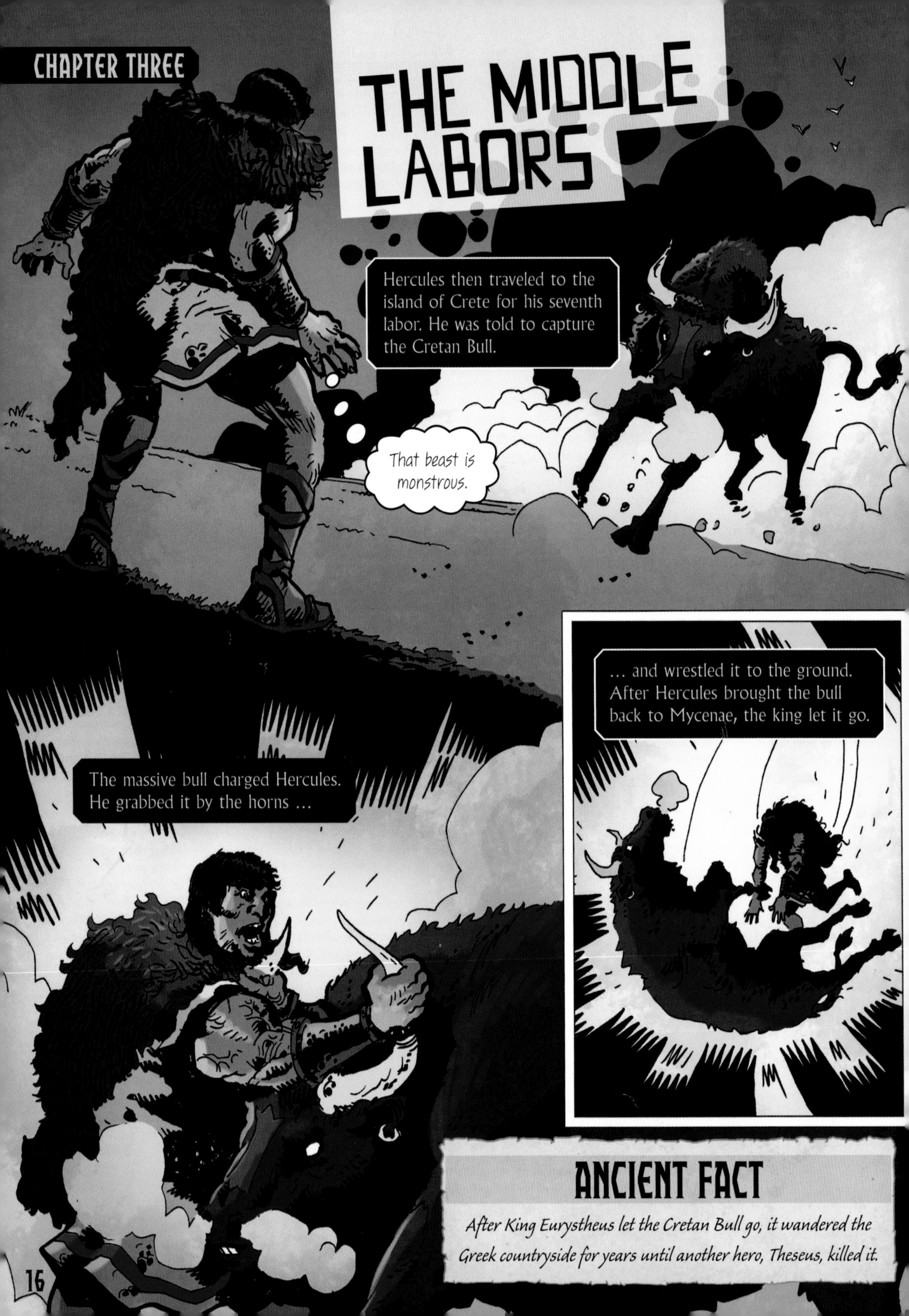

Hercules then traveled to the island of Crete for his seventh labor. He was told to capture the Cretan Bull.
That beast is monstrous.
The massive bull charged Hercules. He grabbed it by the horns ...
... and wrestled it to the ground. After Hercules brought the bull back to Mycenae, the king let it go.

ANCIENT FACT

After King Eurystheus let the Cretan Bull go, it wandered the Greek countryside for years until another hero, Theseus, killed it.

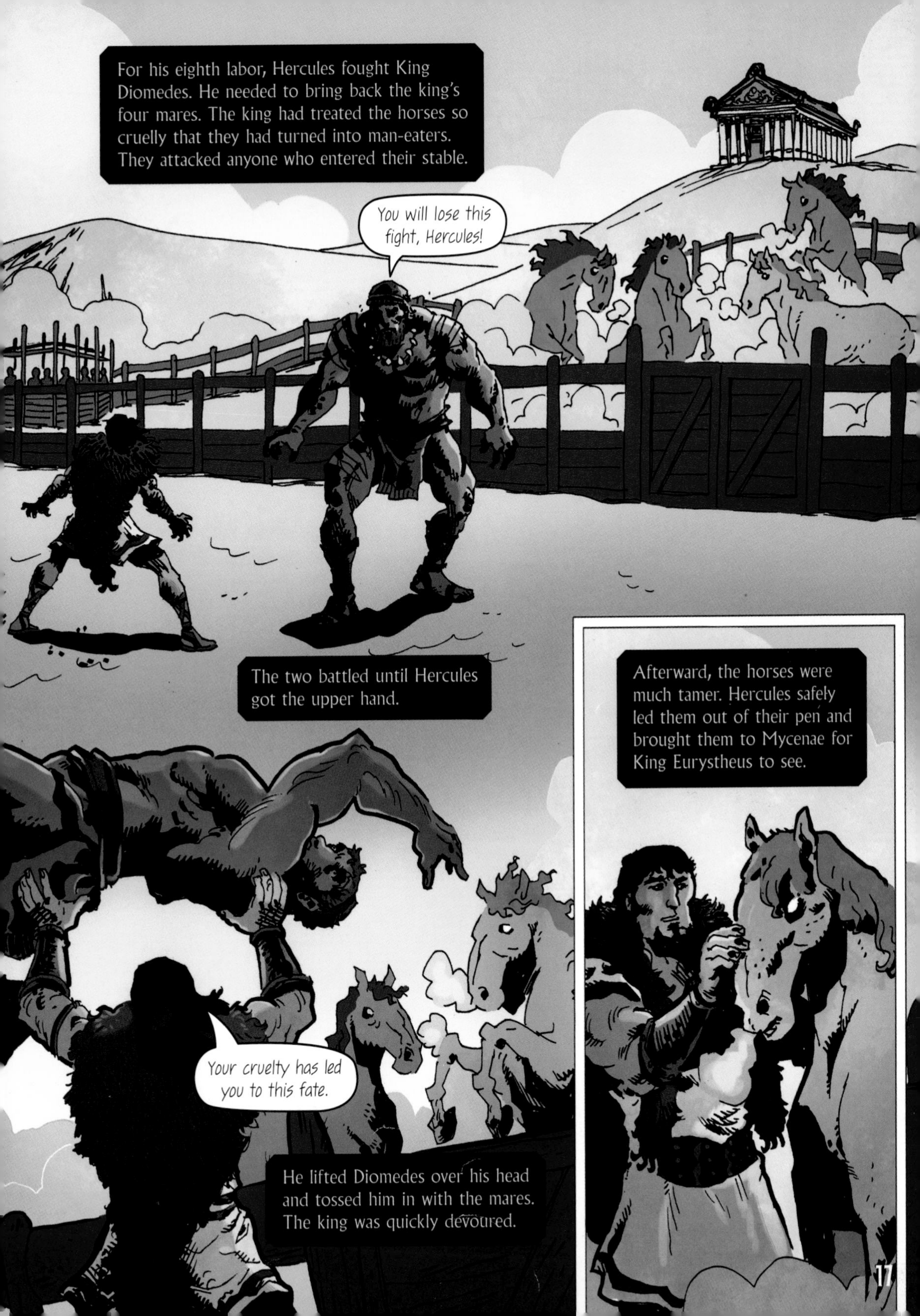
For his eighth labor, Hercules fought King Diomedes. He needed to bring back the king's four mares. The king had treated the horses so cruelly that they had turned into man-eaters. They attacked anyone who entered their stable.
You will lose this fight, Hercules!
The two battled until Hercules got the upper hand.
Your cruelty has led you to this fate.
He lifted Diomedes over his head and tossed him in with the mares. The king was quickly devoured.
Afterward, the horses were much tamer. Hercules safely led them out of their pen and brought them to Mycenae for King Eurystheus to see.

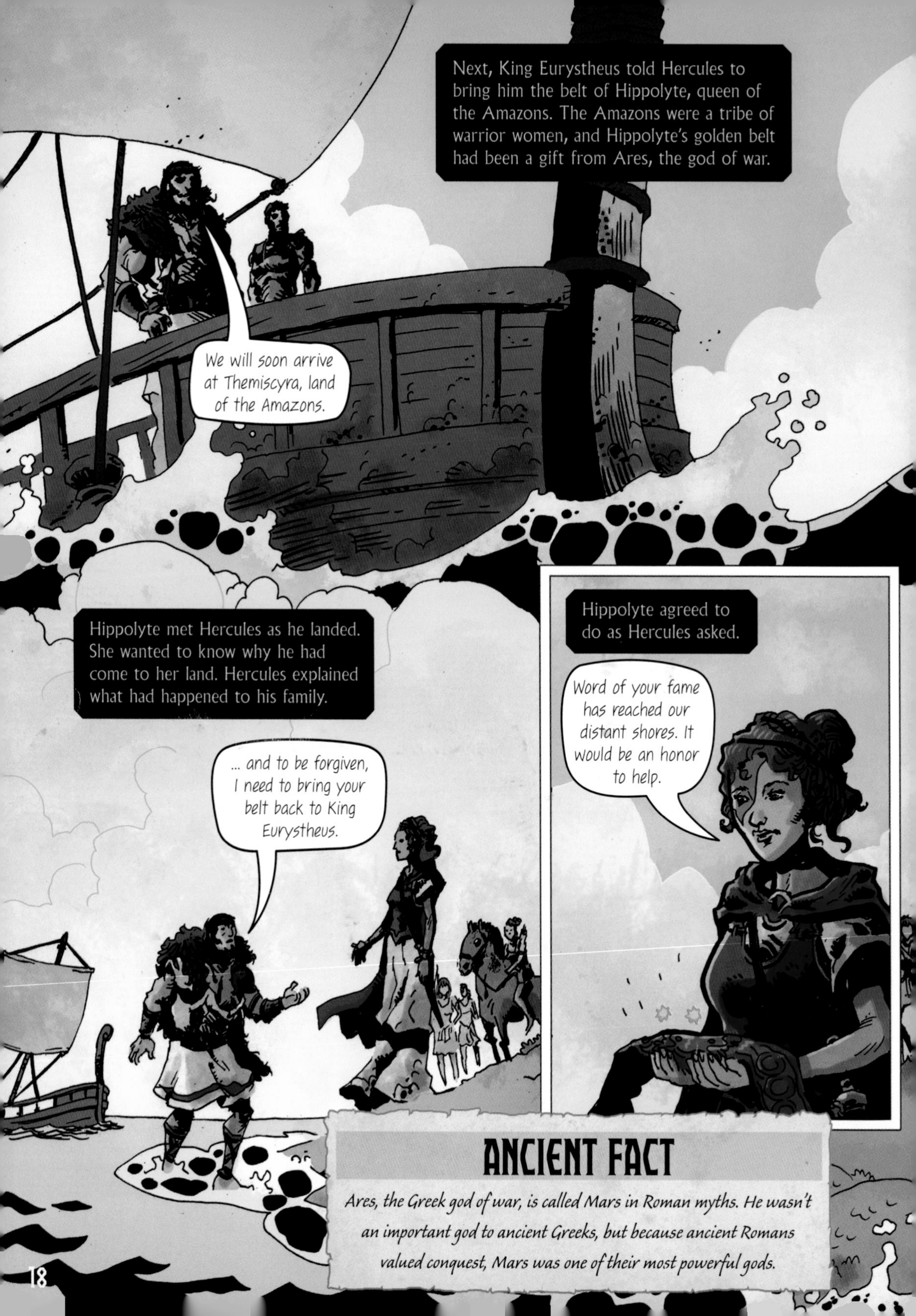
Next, King Eurystheus told Hercules to bring him the belt of Hippolyte, queen of the Amazons. The Amazons were a tribe of warrior women, and Hippolyte's golden belt had been a gift from Ares, the god of war.
We will soon arrive at Themiscyra, land of the Amazons.
Hippolyte met Hercules as he landed. She wanted to know why he had come to her land. Hercules explained what had happened to his family.
... and to be forgiven, I need to bring your belt back to King Eurystheus.
Hippolyte agreed to do as Hercules asked.
Word of your fame has reached our distant shores. It would be an honor to help.

ANCIENT FACT

Ares, the Greek god of war, is called Mars in Roman myths. He wasn't an important god to ancient Greeks, but because ancient Romans valued conquest, Mars was one of their most powerful gods.

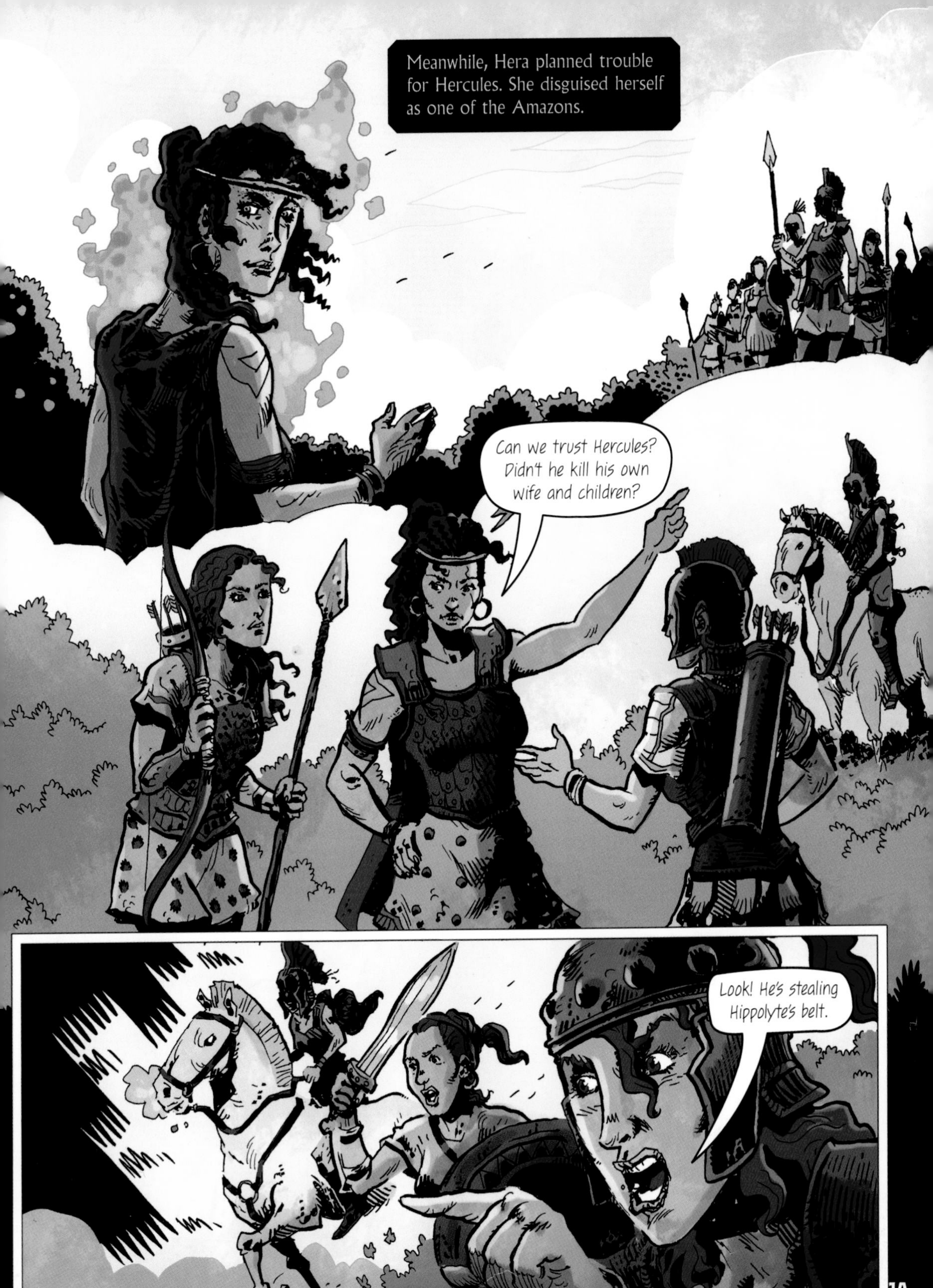
Meanwhile, Hera planned trouble for Hercules. She disguised herself as one of the Amazons.
Can we trust Hercules? Didn't he kill his own wife and children?
Look! He's stealing Hippolyte's belt.

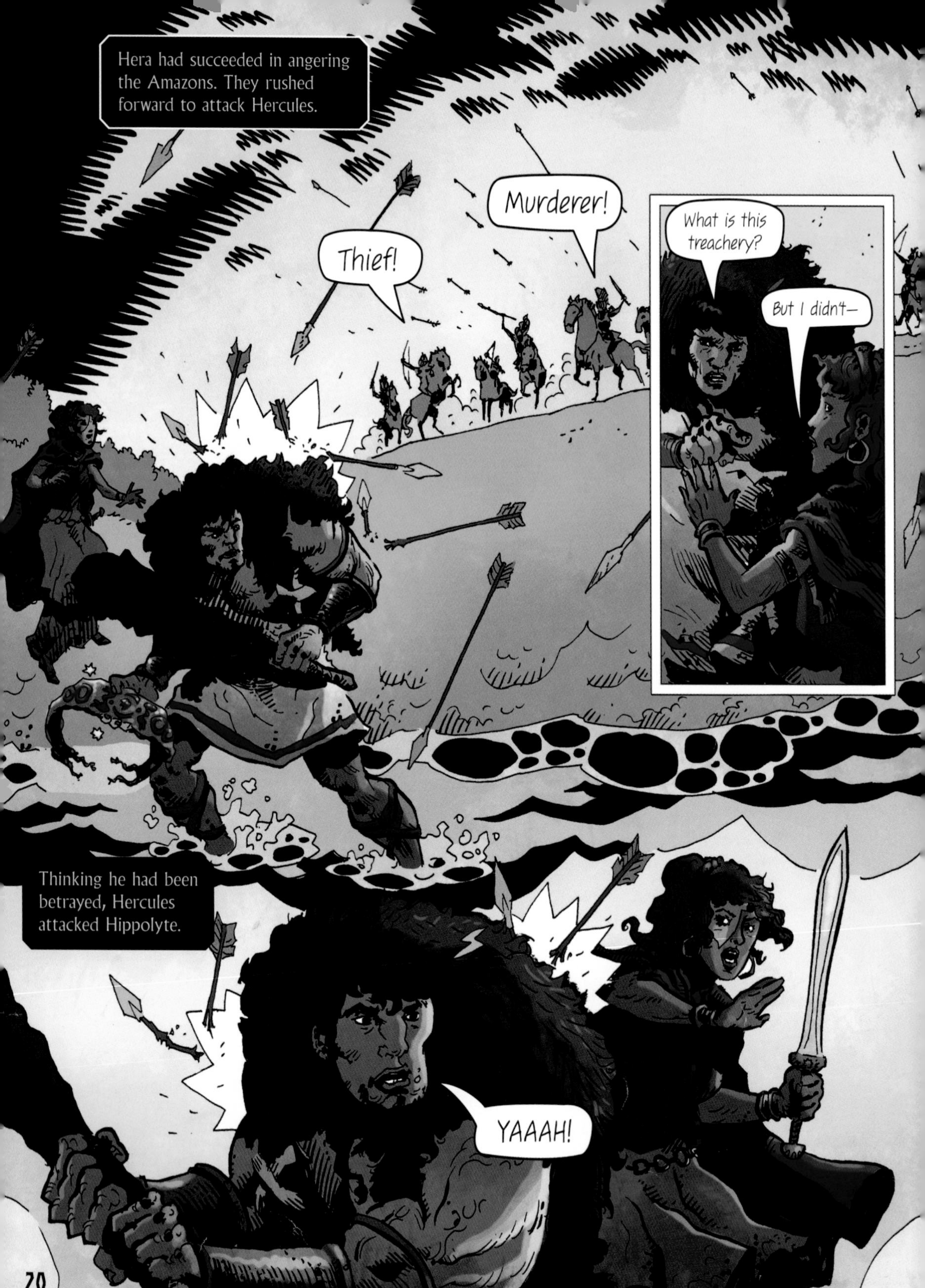
Hera had succeeded in angering the Amazons. They rushed forward to attack Hercules.
Thief!
Murderer!
What is this treachery?
But I didn't—
Thinking he had been betrayed, Hercules attacked Hippolyte.
YAAAH!

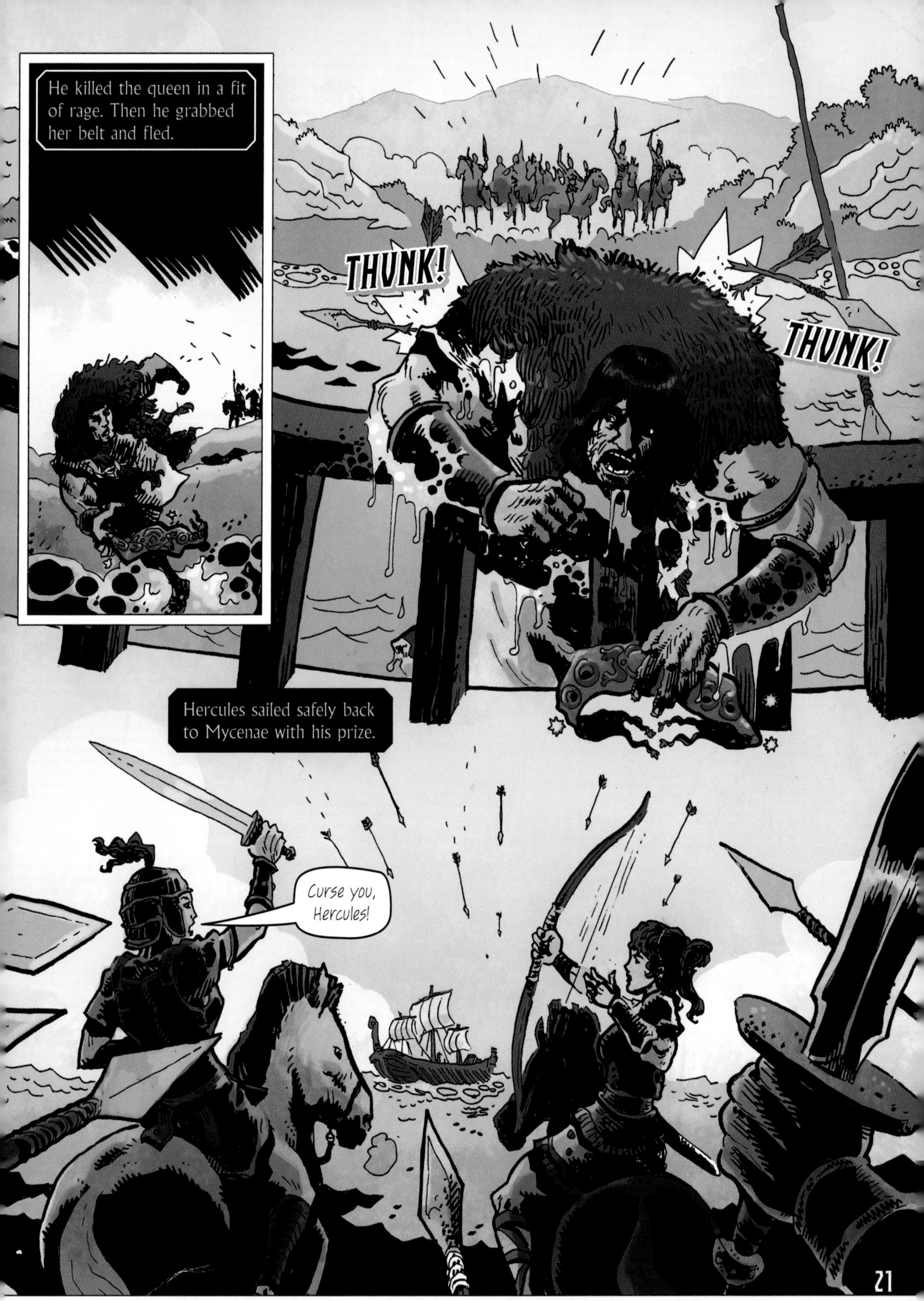
He killed the queen in a fit of rage. Then he grabbed her belt and fled.
THUNK!
THUNK!
Hercules sailed safely back to Mycenae with his prize.
Curse you, Hercules!

CHAPTER FOUR

THE FINAL LABORS

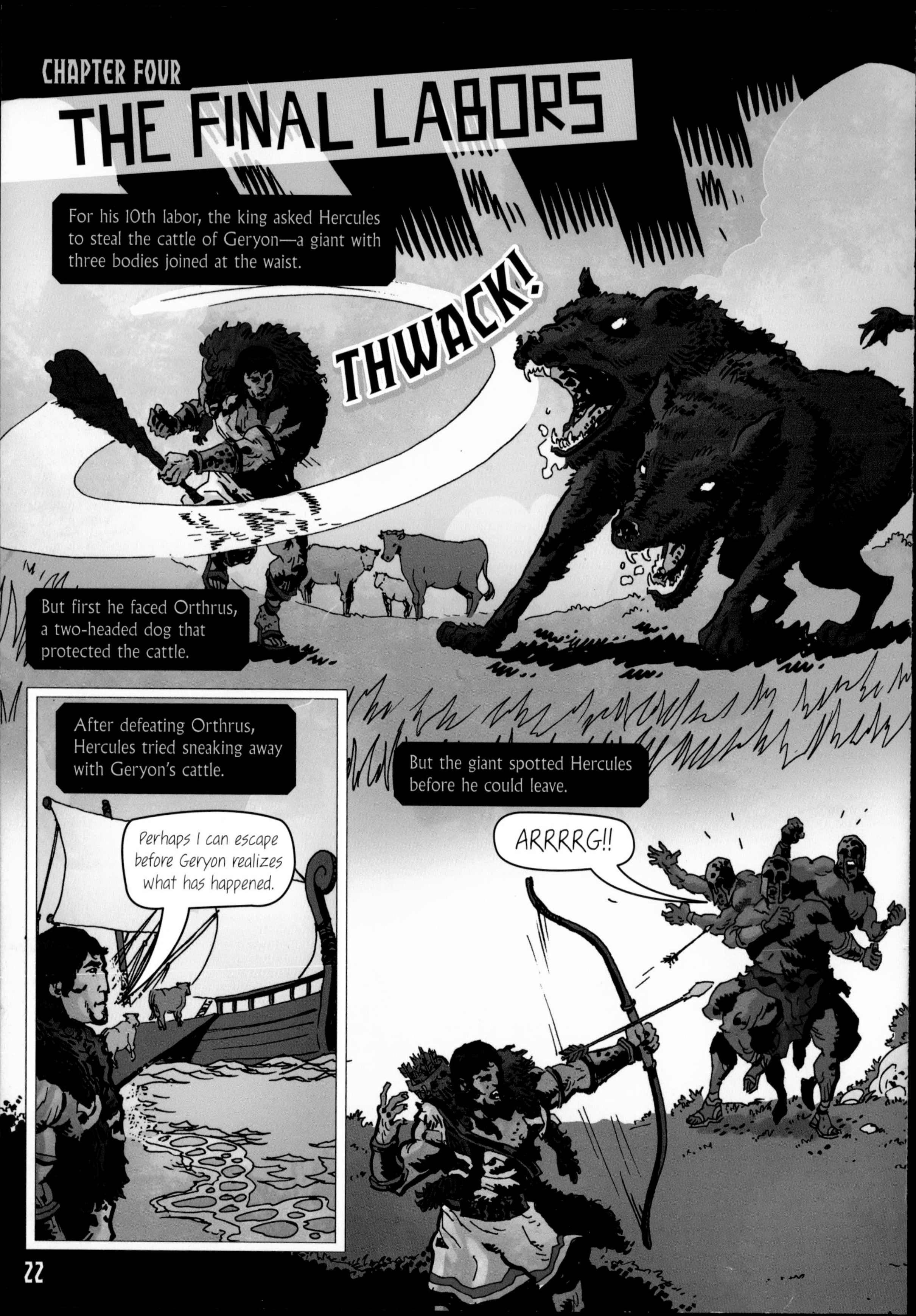
For his 10th labor, the king asked Hercules to steal the cattle of Geryon—a giant with three bodies joined at the waist.
THWACK!
But first he faced Orthrus, a two-headed dog that protected the cattle.
After defeating Orthrus, Hercules tried sneaking away with Geryon's cattle.
Perhaps I can escape before Geryon realizes what has happened.
But the giant spotted Hercules before he could leave.
ARRRRG!!

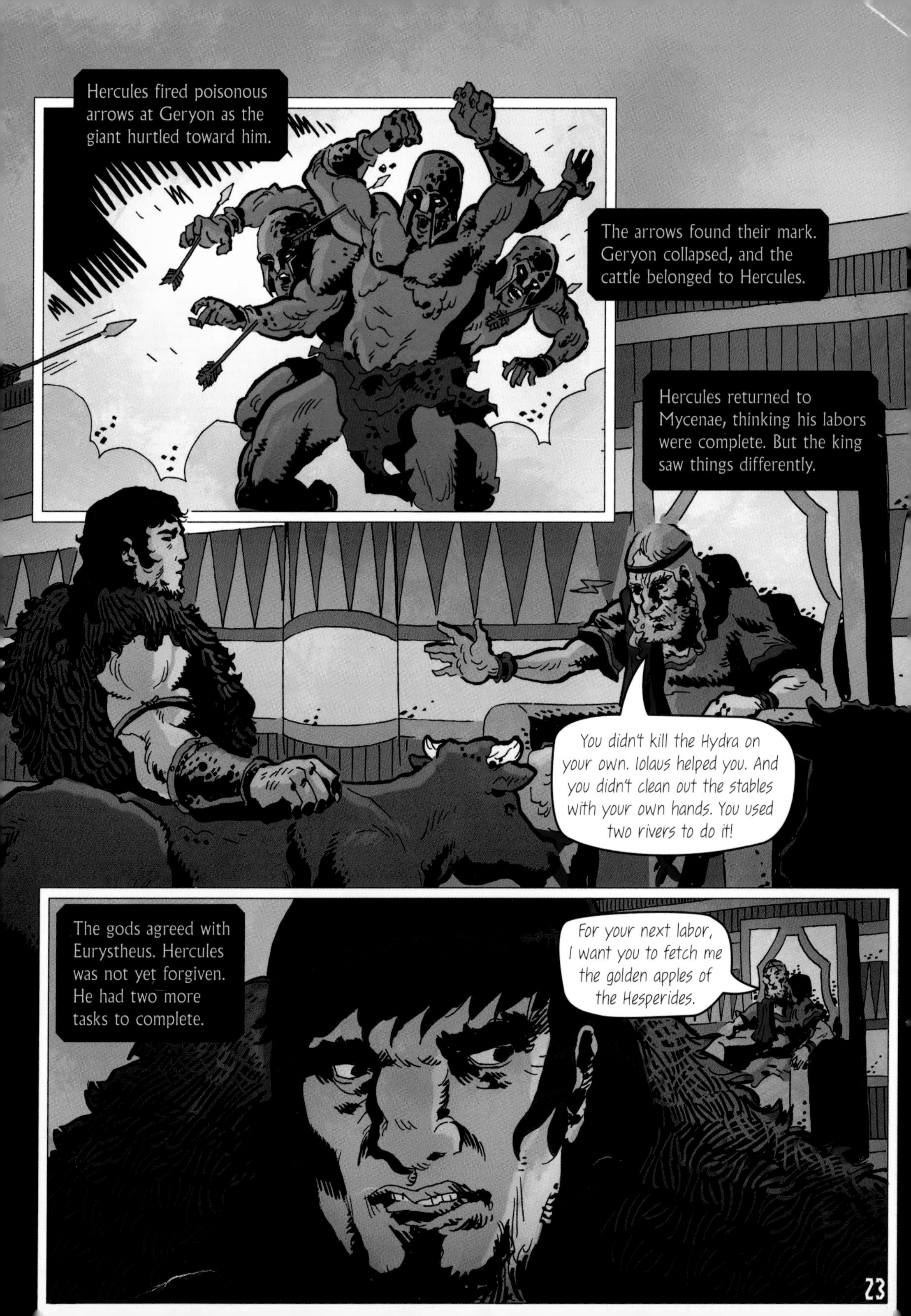
Hercules fired poisonous arrows at Geryon as the giant hurtled toward him.
The arrows found their mark. Geryon collapsed, and the cattle belonged to Hercules.
Hercules returned to Mycenae, thinking his labors were complete. But the king saw things differently.
You didn't kill the Hydra on your own. Iolaus helped you. And you didn't clean out the stables with your own hands. You used two rivers to do it!
The gods agreed with Eurystheus. Hercules was not yet forgiven. He had two more tasks to complete.
For your next labor, I want you to fetch me the golden apples of the Hesperides.

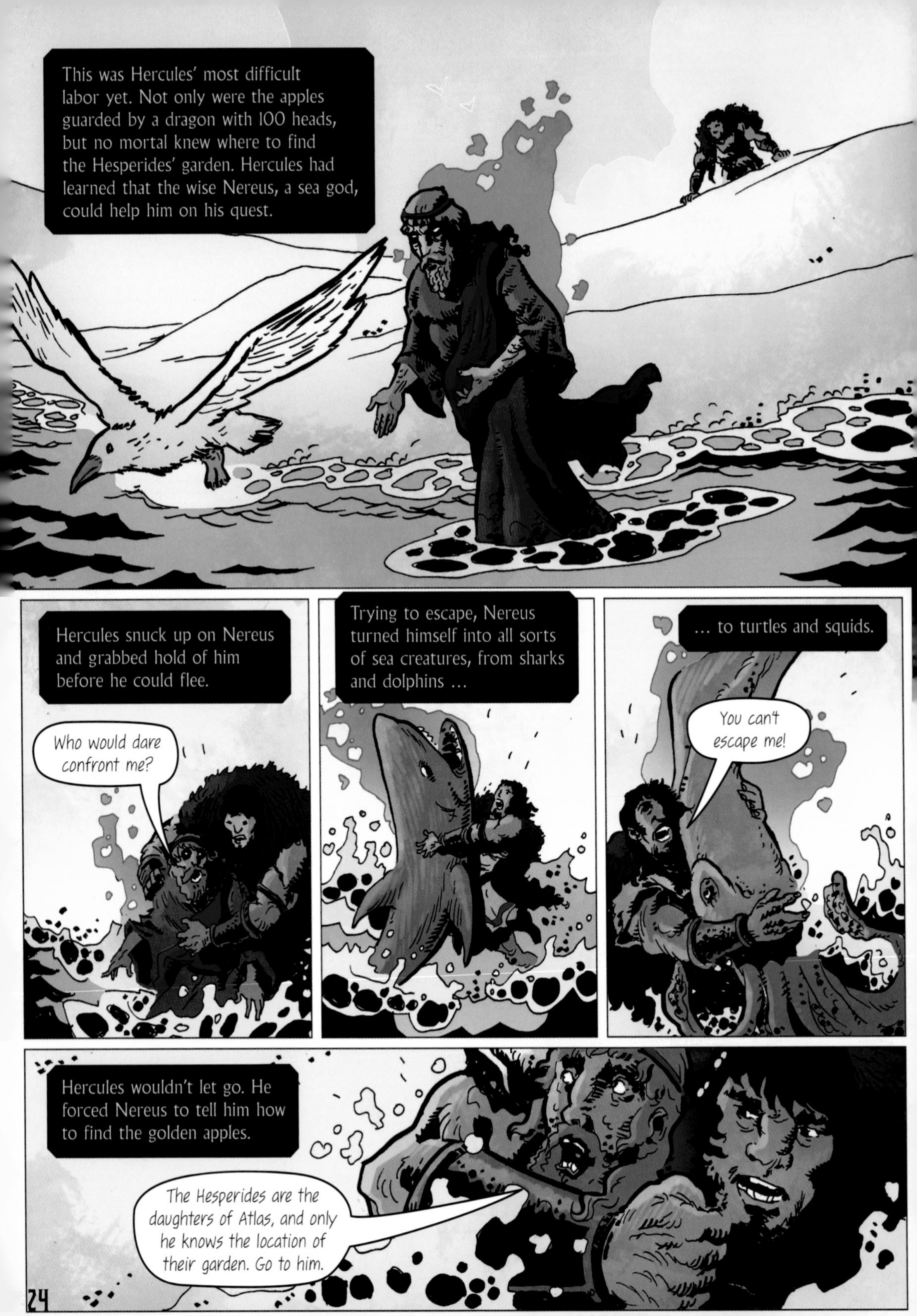
This was Hercules' most difficult labor yet. Not only were the apples guarded by a dragon with 100 heads, but no mortal knew where to find the Hesperides' garden. Hercules had learned that the wise Nereus, a sea god, could help him on his quest.
Hercules snuck up on Nereus and grabbed hold of him before he could flee.
Who would dare confront me?
Trying to escape, Nereus turned himself into all sorts of sea creatures, from sharks and dolphins ...
... to turtles and squids.
You can't escape me!
Hercules wouldn't let go. He forced Nereus to tell him how to find the golden apples.
The Hesperides are the daughters of Atlas, and only he knows the location of their garden. Go to him.

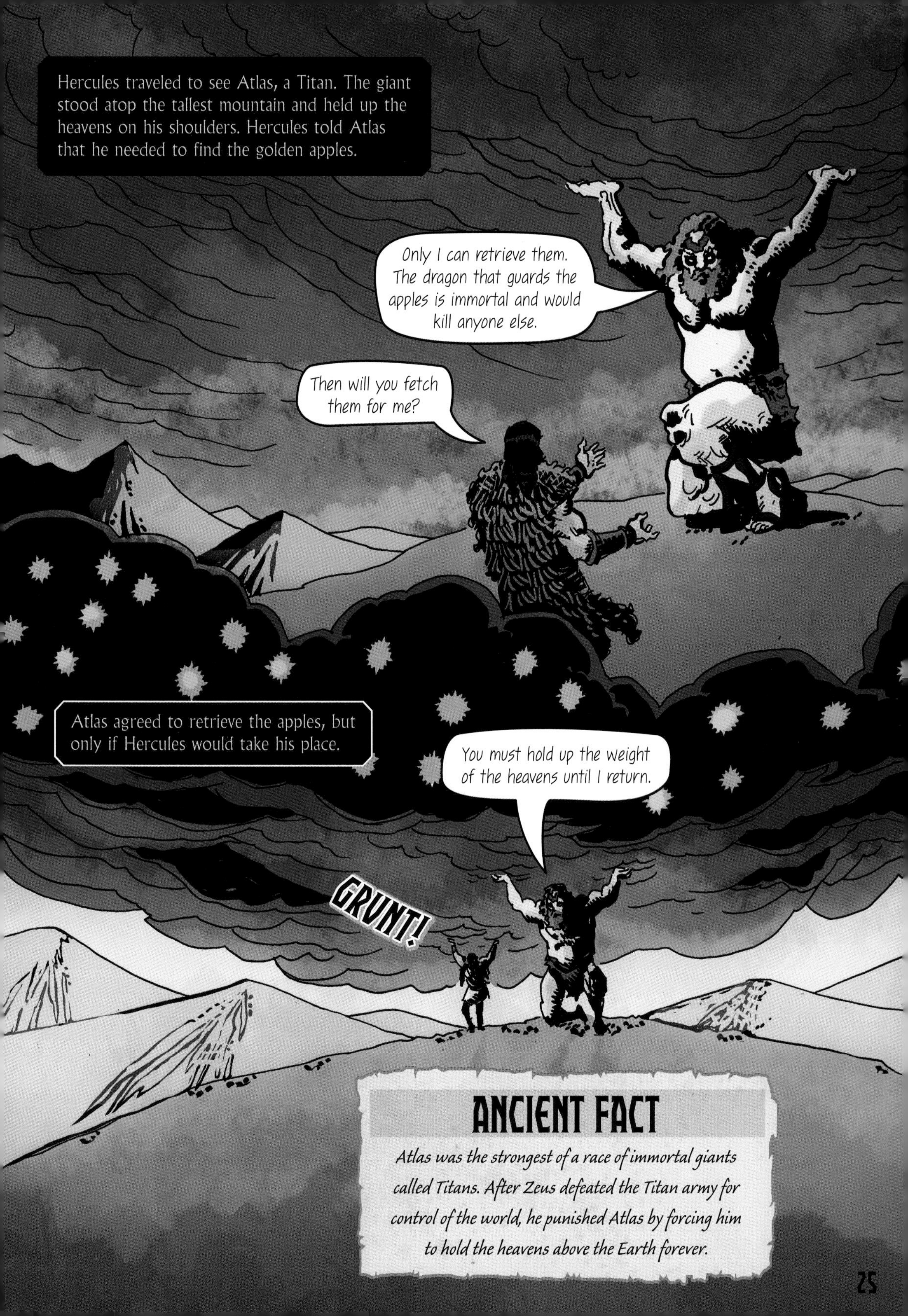
Hercules traveled to see Atlas, a Titan. The giant stood atop the tallest mountain and held up the heavens on his shoulders. Hercules told Atlas that he needed to find the golden apples.
Only I can retrieve them. The dragon that guards the apples is immortal and would kill anyone else.
Then will you fetch them for me?
Atlas agreed to retrieve the apples, but only if Hercules would take his place.
You must hold up the weight of the heavens until I return.
GRUNT!

ANCIENT FACT

Atlas was the strongest of a race of immortal giants called Titans. After Zeus defeated the Titan army for control of the world, he punished Atlas by forcing him to hold the heavens above the Earth forever.

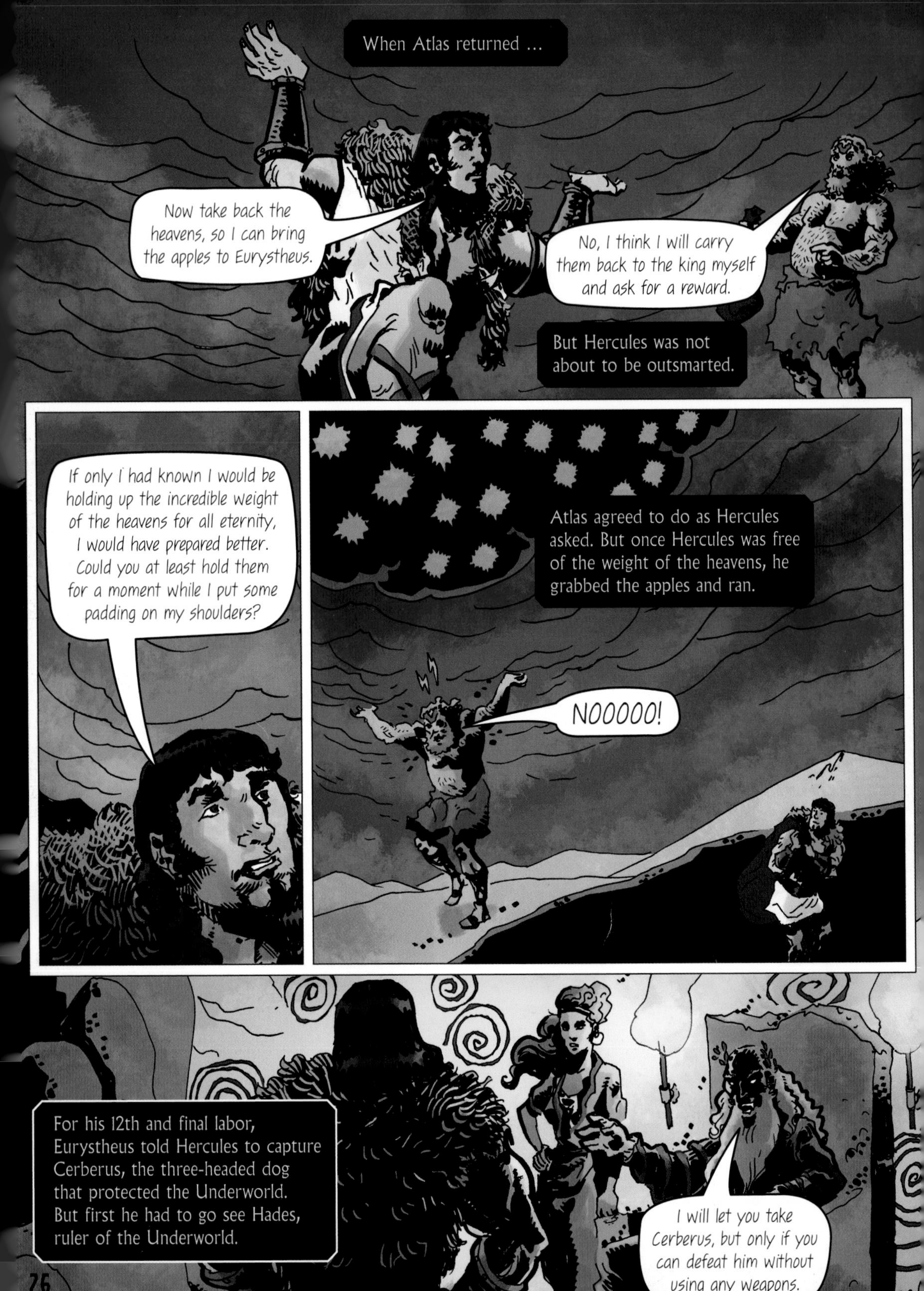

When Atlas returned ...
Now take back the heavens, so I can bring the apples to Eurystheus.
No, I think I will carry them back to the king myself and ask for a reward.
But Hercules was not about to be outsmarted.
If only I had known I would be holding up the incredible weight of the heavens for all eternity, I would have prepared better. Could you at least hold them for a moment while I put some padding on my shoulders?
Atlas agreed to do as Hercules asked. But once Hercules was free of the weight of the heavens, he grabbed the apples and ran.
NOOOOO!
For his 12th and final labor, Eurystheus told Hercules to capture Cerberus, the three-headed dog that protected the Underworld. But first he had to go see Hades, ruler of the Underworld.
I will let you take Cerberus, but only if you can defeat him without using any weapons.

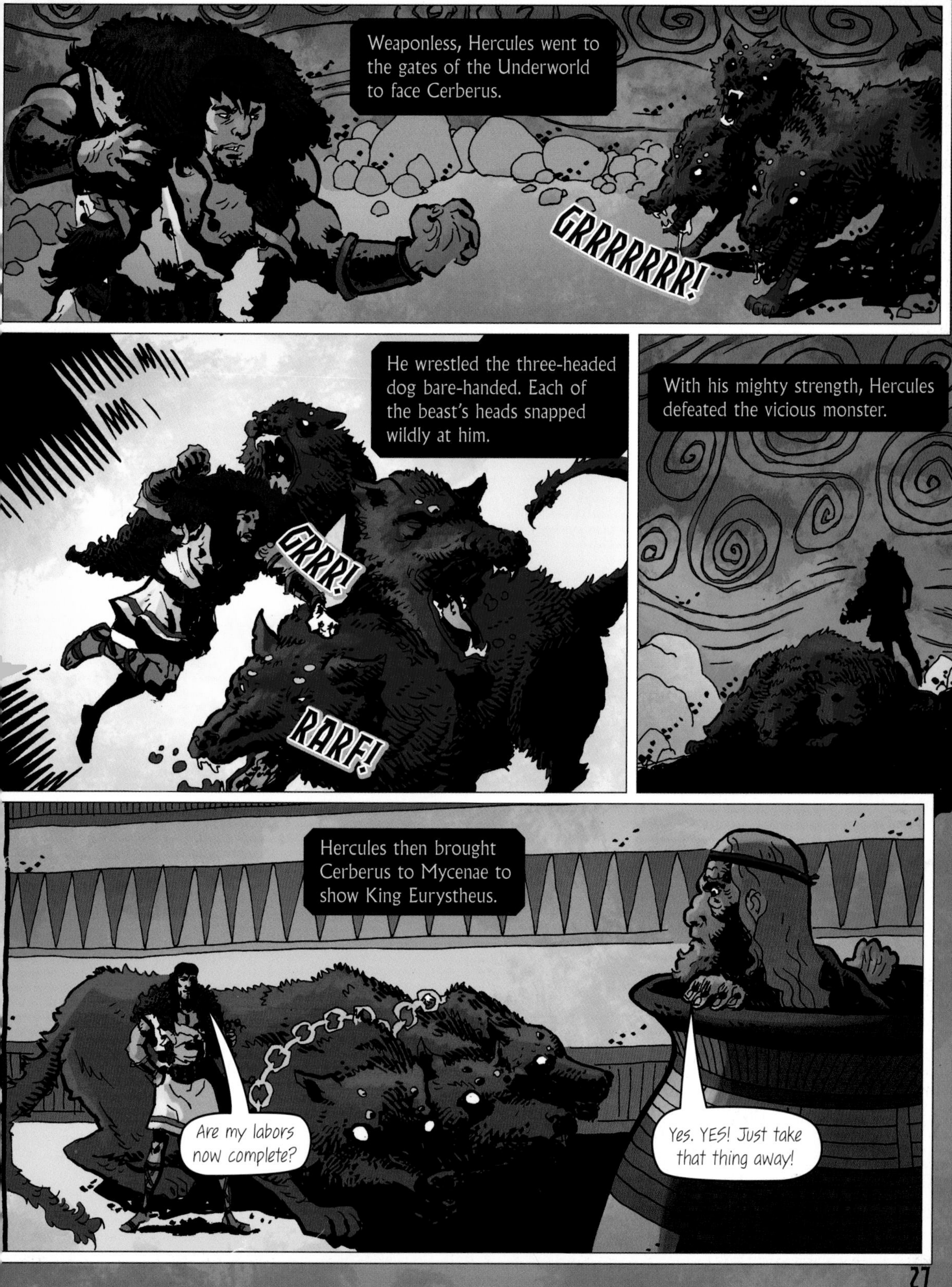
Weaponless, Hercules went to the gates of the Underworld to face Cerberus.
GRRRRRRRR!
He wrestled the three-headed dog bare-handed. Each of the beast's heads snapped wildly at him.
GRRR!
RARF!
With his mighty strength, Hercules defeated the vicious monster.
Hercules then brought Cerberus to Mycenae to show King Eurystheus.
Are my labors now complete?
Yes. YES! Just take that thing away!

CHAPTER FIVE

THE LEGACY OF HERCULES

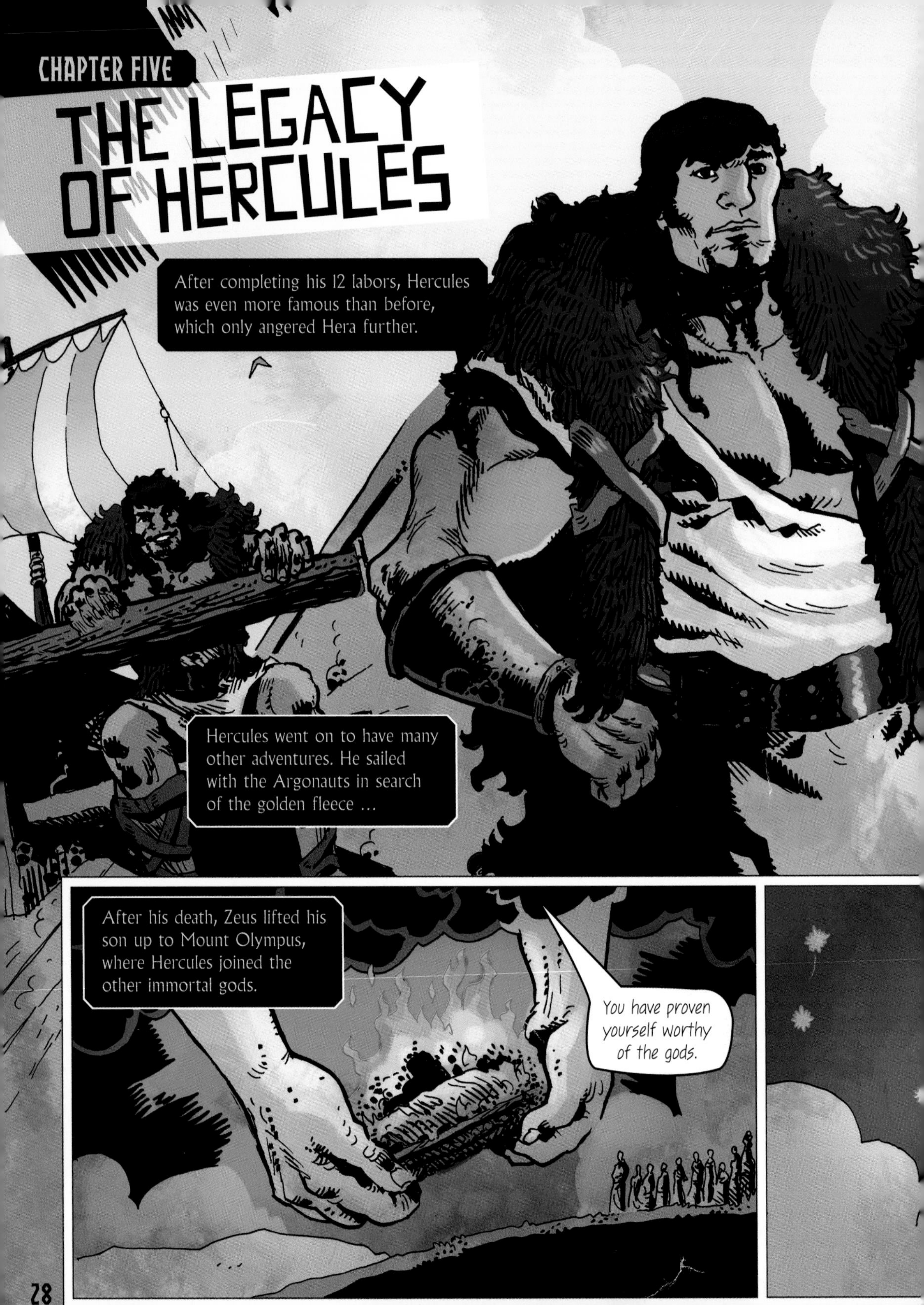
After completing his 12 labors, Hercules was even more famous than before, which only angered Hera further.
Hercules went on to have many other adventures. He sailed with the Argonauts in search of the golden fleece …
After his death, Zeus lifted his son up to Mount Olympus, where Hercules joined the other immortal gods.
You have proven yourself worthy of the gods.

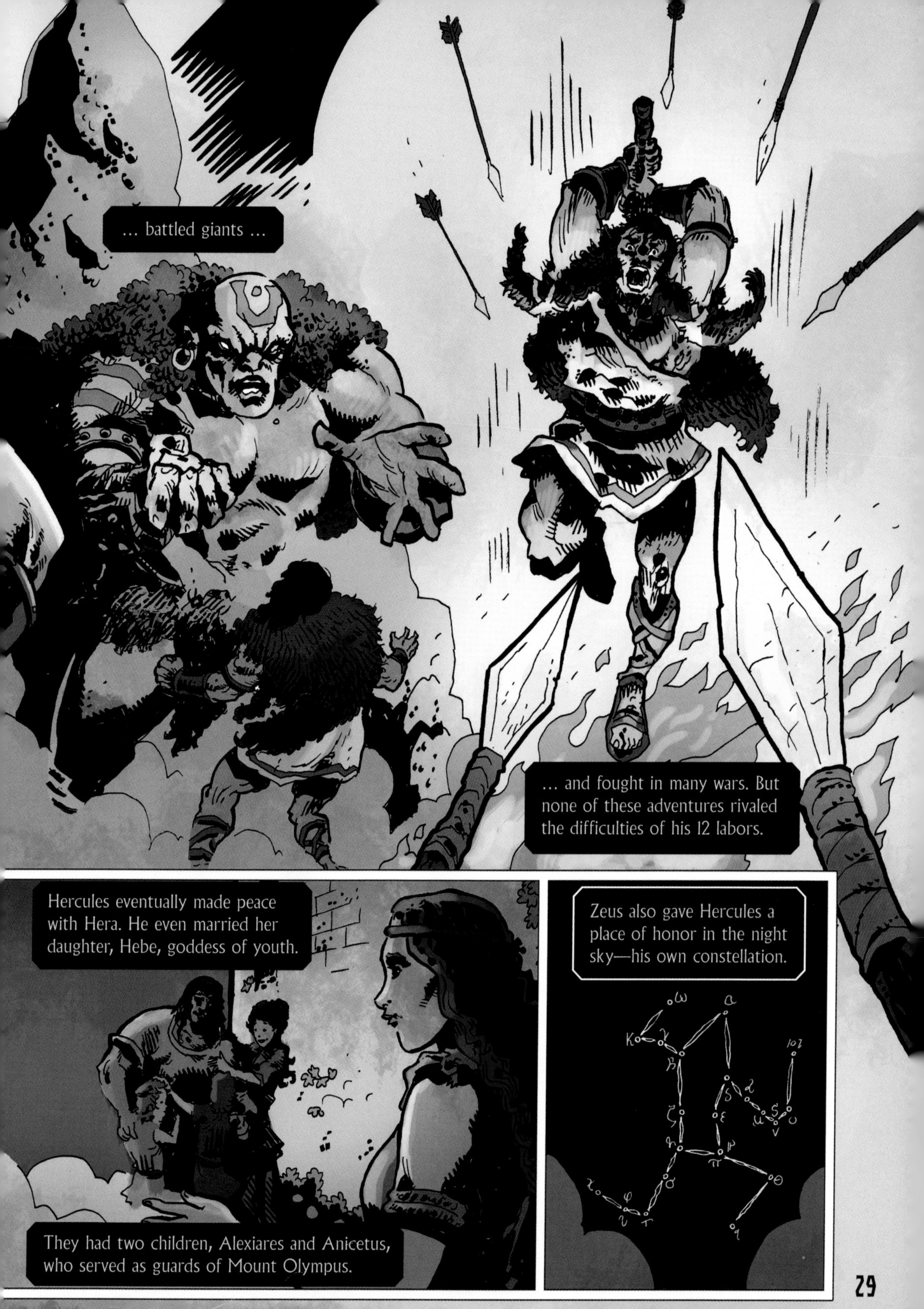
... battled giants ...
... and fought in many wars. But none of these adventures rivaled the difficulties of his 12 labors.
Hercules eventually made peace with Hera. He even married her daughter, Hebe, goddess of youth.
They had two children, Alexiares and Anicetus, who served as guards of Mount Olympus.
Zeus also gave Hercules a place of honor in the night sky—his own constellation.

GLOSSARY

constellation (con-stuh-LAY-shun)—a group of stars that form a pattern; many of the constellations are named after mythical figures

hide (HIDE)—an animal's skin

immortal (i-MOR-tuhl)—able to live forever, such as the gods in myths

invulnerable (in-VUHL-nur-uh-buhl)—impossible to harm

madness (MAD-nuhss)—the state of being mentally ill

mortal (MOR-tuhl)—unable to live forever; people are mortal

oracle (OR-uh-kuhl)—in ancient myths, a person who could interpret the future

quest (KWEST)—a long journey to perform a task or find something

sacred (SAY-krid)—an important religious item

strangle (STRAN-guhl)—to choke to death

underworld (UN-dur-wurld)—the land of the dead in myths

READ MORE

Ford, James. *The Twelve Labors of Hercules*. Ancient Greek Myths. New York: Sandy Creek, 2013.

Hoena, Blake. *Everything Mythology*. National Geographic Kids. Washington, D.C.: National Geographic Children's Books, 2014.

Orr, Tamra. *The Monsters of Hercules*. Monsters in Myth. Hockessin, Del.: Mitchell Lane Publishers, 2011.

O'Shei, Tim. *Bone-Chilling Myths*. Scary Stories. Mankato, Minn.: Capstone Press, 2011.

INTERNET SITES

FactHound offers a safe, fun way to find Internet sites related to this book. All of the sites on FactHound have been researched by our staff.

Here's all you do:

Visit *www.facthound.com*

Type in this code: 9781491420713

Super-cool stuff!

Check out projects, games and lots more at
www.capstonekids.com

INDEX

TITLES IN THIS SET

A GRAPHIC RETELLING
THE 12 LABORS OF
HERCULES

A GRAPHIC RETELLING
JASON
AND THE ARGONAUTS

A GRAPHIC RETELLING
THE VOYAGE OF
ODYSSEUS

A GRAPHIC RETELLING
THE ADVENTURES OF
PERSEUS

A GRAPHIC RETELLING
THESEUS
AND THE MINOTAUR

A GRAPHIC RETELLING
THE
TROJAN WAR

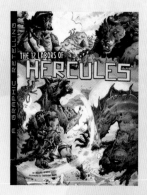

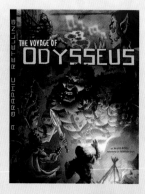